HORTICULTURE PONDER POINTS

BEST READY RECKONER FOR HO/AO/ADH INTERVIEW AND COMPETITIVE EXAMS

MS. D. H. PITHADIA

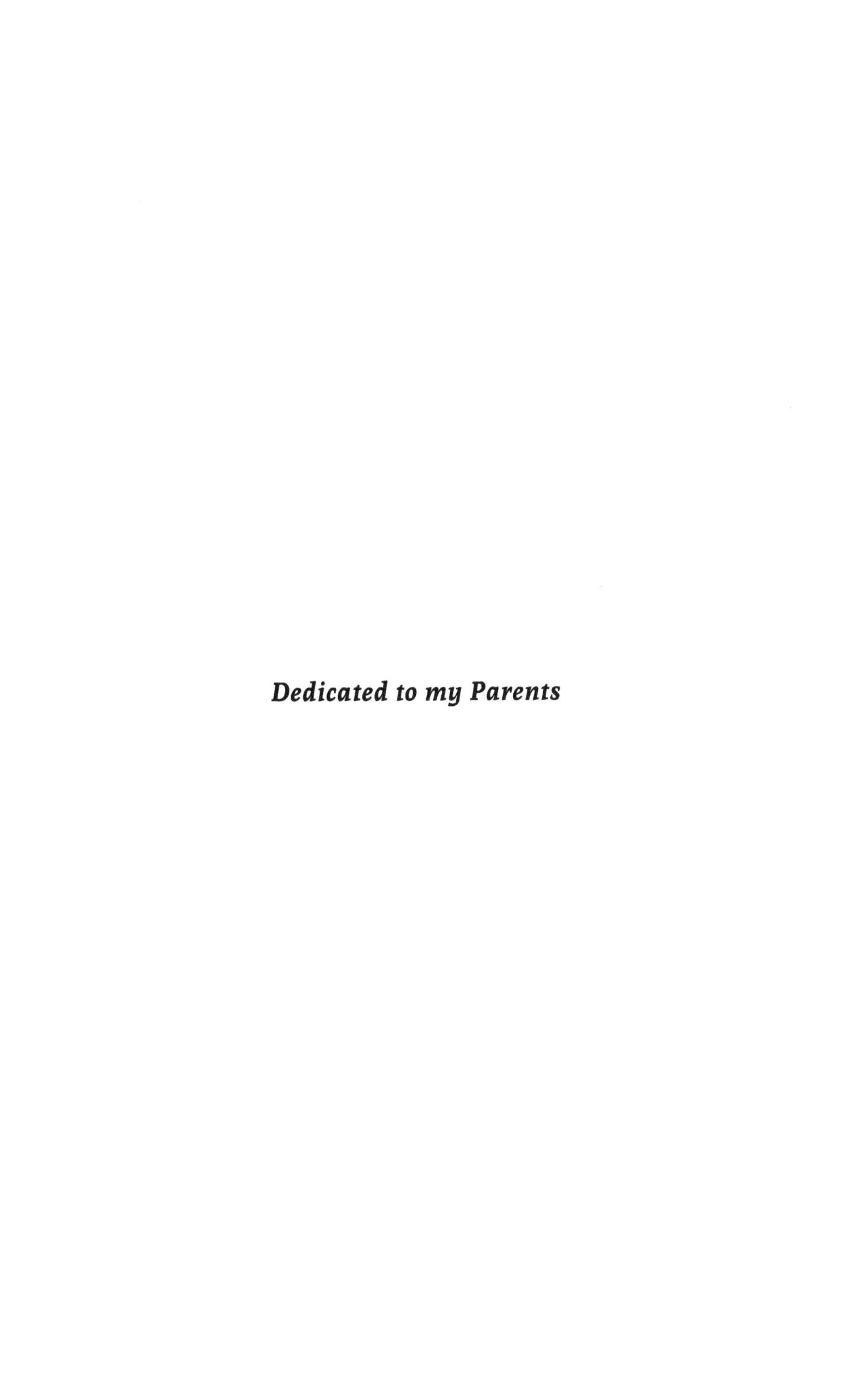

Dedicated to my Parents

Contents

PREFACE

Horticulture is a very vast subject itself. It covers fruits, vegetables, flowers, post-harvest technology and many more. Very interesting thing is that now a days government also expanding their efforts in Horticulture and provide notable supports to the farmers directly and indirectly. To be a part of government to serve the farmers, competitive exams are only way and we have to clear it first. There is some specific exam pattern for each level exams. I have noted here important ponder points about Horticulture. To clear the Horticulture officer, Assistant Director of Horticulture interviews and exam this book is very important. Here I mention all the practical practices and applied questions about the Horticulture which are mainly asked by interviewers. This book contains modern Agriculture concepts, Horticulture pest and disease with field level solutions, applied agriculture points, and government schemes. This book proves best interview preparation book for government exam students.

Author name: Ms. D. H. Pithadia

Date: 25th Jan. 2022

ACKNOWLEDGEMENTS

The word is better place to thank people who wand to develope others. Thanks to each and every people who shared their precious time for others bright future. Thanks to all individual who helped me and support me for step to step process.

I want to start by thanking my parents and little sister who always stand for me as fighters. As we move further I would like to thanks my friends.

Additionally, my special thanks to Dr. M. V. Patel and Mr. P. D. Golakiya for always help me to overcom my challenges.

Lastly, I like to thanks my almighty God for everything.

I

Modern Agriculture

MICRO IRRIGATION

- Benefits of Micro Irrigation:

1. Generally, reduce the climate related yield risk resulting from water stress
2. Micro Irrigation increase the efficiency of water, you can utilize per drop of water
3. Allows for flexibility in timing & amount of applied water
4. In micro irrigation less water applied so it reduces nutrient leaching also.
5. Protect small horticulture crops from freeze
6. Surface crusting is reducing
7. Joint management of irrigation and fertilization can be possible effectively

- Scheme involved in Micro Irrigation:

1. PradhanMantri Sinchay Yojna (2015)

- Types of micro irrigation:

1. Drip Irrigation
2. Sprinkler Irrigation
3. Spray Irrigation
4. Subsurface Irrigation

5. Bubbler Irrigation

- Irrigation Efficiency

- Application Efficiency:

    - Surface method: 40–70%
    - Sprinkler method: 60–80%
    - Drip method: 90%

- Surface water moisture evaporation:

    - Surface method: 30–40%
    - Sprinkler method: 30–40%
    - Drip method: 20-25%

- Overall efficiency:

    - Surface method: 30-35%
    - Sprinkle method: 50-70%
    - Drip method: 80-90%

ℬ

FARM MECHANIZATION

- Farm mechanization having both pros and cons but ultimately farm mechanization is useful for the farmers and to get high income with less efforts farm mechanization is blessing for farmers.
- Let's take an example, If farmer is doing sowing operation of Soybean in 1 ha. of land with tractor and seed cum fertilizer drill with 9 row where row to row distance is 30 cm. If sowing is done at speed of 2.5 km/hr, it will take almost 2 labors and 1.5 hr. for sowing with the cost of 800-1000 Rs./ha.
- If the same farmer not using any farm mechanization and doing same practices with bullock pair then 1 pair bullock will need total seven person for putting seed and fertilizer. It will take 2.5 to 3 hr. and cost will be 2500-3000Rs./ha. And also you will not get perfect row to row spacing

and uneven seed distribution.

- So this is the difference in farming with farm mechanization.

- Benefits of Farm Mechanization:

1. Higher productivity with same piece of land
2. Reduce time and cost of farm operation
3. High efficiency of work
4. Timely operation

- Farm Mechanization blessing for farmers/country or not?

    - Population of the country is increasing at the rate of 2.2% per year. Steps have to be taken to arrange food and fiber for such large population by adoption intensive farming in the country. Intensive farming requires machines on farm. So as per my point of view farm mechanization is needful/blessing for farmers.

- Social Prospective of Farm Mechanization:

    - A large number of females and children used to work on farm, so with the farm mechanization females are working at home and children can go to schools. So as social view it will be beneficial for society also.

- Scheme supports Farm Mechanization:

1. Agriculture Mechanization Promotion Scheme

   Objective: Reduce air pollution

ஐ

HDP AND UHDP

- High Density Planting and Ultra High Density Planting
- First planted in Europe in the year of 1960
- HDP is one of improved production technology to achieve the objective of enhance productivity

- HDP is balance between vegetative and reproductive system without impairing the plant health
- As a part of National Horticulture Mission, the department of horticulture in Madurai has introduced UHDP in Mango

- Principle of HDP:

1. Best use of vertical and horizontal space per unit time
2. To get maximum possible return per unit of inputs and resources

- Factors affect HDP:

1. Cultivars
2. Planting system
3. Planting material
4. Nutrition and moisture
5. Economics of production

- How to control tree size in HDP?

1. Use of dwarf scion cultivar:

    - Ex. Mango- Amrapali, Papaya- Pusha Nanha, Banana- Dwarf cavandish, Sapota- PKM 1, PKM 3, Cherrymeteor, North star

2. Use of dwarf rootstock:

    - Ex. Apple- M9, M26, M27, Pear- Quince C, Cherry- Pixy, Ber- *Ziziyphus rotundifolia*, Citrus- Citrangequat, Guava- *Pisidium friedrichsthalianum*

3. Training and Pruning
4. Use of growth retardant

    - Ex. CCC, Paclobutrazole

5. Induction of viral infection

    - Not adopted commercially

- Planting system:

1. Square and triangle in Mango, Banana, Papaya
2. Hedge row in Apple and Pineapple

- Constrains of HDP:
- Lack of standardization and technology
- High initial establishment cost
- Lack of dwarf rootstock
- High incidence of some disease in HDP. Ex. Sigatoka leaf spot and Fingertip in Banana

GREENHOUSE CULTIVATION

- Greenhouse Design:

1. Greenhouse structure should be covered with transparent material
2. Controlled environment condition should be there
3. Favorable micro climate available for crop production
4. Control the temperature, light, CO_2 level, water, and Relative Humidity available for crop

- Cost Involved:

1. Less expensive without fan & pad GH Rs. 300 to 500/m^2
2. Medium cost with pad & fan Greenhouse without automation Rs. 800 to 1100/m^2
3. Expensive Greenhouse fully controlled and automatic Rs. 2000 to 3500/m^2

- Classification of Greenhouse based on cost:

1. Low cost or Low tech.
2. Medium tech.
3. Hi-tech

- Classification on basis of structure:

1. Quonset
2. Curved roof
3. Gable roof

- Poly house: Crops grown in open field are exposed to vivid environmental condition, attack of insect and pest provide more stable environment

  - Naturally Ventilated
  - Environmental Controlled

- Guideline for greenhouse structure:

1. Ultra violet resistant low density polyethylene (UVLDPE) with 200 micron thickness is sufficient
2. Greenhouse location should avoid falling of shadow on the adjacent. The movement of shadow of the gutter across the greenhouse
3. Greenhous direction should be east to west. However, wind direction and latitude also consider
4. Greenhous size- 50*50 m
5. Space between two greenhouses is should be 10-15 m
6. Height: 5m for 50*50 m
7. Side ventilation should 2 m width and roof ventilation 1 m width

- Media used in greenhouse:
- Commercially available materials like peat, sphagnum moss, vermiculite, perlite and locally available material like sand, red soil, manure, compost and rise husk

HYDROPONICS – AQUAPONICS - AEROPONICS

- Hydroponics: Growing of plant without soil. Plants are grown in other medias such as water. Nutrients are supplied through fertilizer added in the watering process.

- Aquaponics: Plants are grown without soil. Primarily in water, where nutrients are supplied from the byproducts of fish. Plants reciprocate the favor by filtering the water.
- Aeroponics: Aeroponics is the process of growing plants in an air or mist environment without use of soil.

Hydroponics	Aeroponics
Growing of plants in nutrient enrich water and without soil	Growing of plants without soil but root are exposed to air
Root of plants exposed to nutrient rich water	Root of plants exposed to nutrient rich mist
Require huge water supply as compare to Aeroponics	Require less water
Chemically inert media is used to hold the plant (Clay, Sand, etc)	No such media is used to hold plant
Less cost require- cheap model	Comparatively expensive
Support more variety of plants	Majorly olives and citrus plants

Enter Caption

ꕥ

USE OF SPACE TECHNOLOGY IN AGRICULTURE

- Ministry of Agriculture and farmers' welfare use in Agriculture.
- Space technology used in crop production and forecasting.
- The department of Agriculture and farmers welfare develop center for forecasting, soil and land use survey which use satellite data.
- Department using space technology in different programed and forecasting. Agriculture output using space technology.
- Agro metrology and land base observation used in many scheme such as FASAL, CHAMAN and NADAMS for area mapping and intensification, geo tagging of infrastructure and assets created under RKVY and crop Insurance.
- Department of Agriculture and farmers' welfare has launched KISAN project space technology used in PMFBY.

II

Vegetable Crop Capsule

Vegetables are simply edible portion of a plant. Different plant parts are eaten as vegetables like leaves, stem, root, tubers, etc. Vegetables are rich source of many nutrients like potassium, vitamin A, vitamin C, dietary fiber, folic acid etc. Let's see some details about vegetable crops.

Crop	Sowing time	Seed Rate	Planting Distance		Seeds/gm	Production	Duration (Days)
			Plant to plant	Row to Row			
Tomato	June-Sept Nov-Dec Mar-April	40-60 g/acre	30-60 cm	150-200 cm	300	15-25 t/acre	120-140
Chilli	June-Sept Nov-Feb	60-80 g/acre	60 cm	120 cm	150-200	Green: 15-20 t/acre Red: 6-8 t/acre	140-160
Brinjal	Mar-April June-Sept Nov-Dec	60-70 g/acre	60 cm	150 cm	200-250	20-30 t/acre	90-110
Cabbage	May-Aug July-Aug	100 g/acre	30-60 cm	30-60 cm	250-300	16-20 t/acre	90-110
Cauliflower	May-Aug	100 g/acre	30-60 cm	30-60 cm	250-350	16-20 t/acre	110-120
Okra	Feb-May June-Sept	2.5-3 kg/acre	30 cm	60 cm	15	50-60 qtl/acre	160-170
Watermelon	Jan-Mar	350 g/acre	30-45 cm	6-8 ft	10	20-30 t/acre	110-120
Muskmelon	Jan-Mar	250-300 g/acre	60 cm	150 cm	30	20-30 t/acre	110-120
Cucumber	Jan-Mar June-July	200-250 g/acre	60 cm	120-150 cm	30-40	10-15 t/acre	100-120
Bitter Gourd	Jan-Mar June-July	300 g/acre	60 cm	150-180 cm	6-7	10-15 t/acre	110-120
Bottle Gourd	Feb-Sept	300 g/acre	60 cm	150-180 cm	6-7	20-25 t/acre	100-120
Ridge Gourd	May-Aug	350 g/acre	60 cm	120-150 cm	10	15-20 t/acre	100-120

Sponge Gourd	Dec-Feb	300 g/acre	60 cm	120-150 cm	12	15-20 t/acre	90-110
Mustard	Sept-Oct	2-2.5 kg/acre	60 cm	30 cm	-	7-10 t/acre	100-130
Cumin	Oct-Nov	5-6 kg/acre	60 cm	30 cm	-		100-120
Gram	Oct-Nov	40 kg/acre	60 cm	30 cm	-		100-120
Soybean	June-July	40 kg/acre	30-45 cm	10-5 cm	8-10	10-15 qtl/acre	90-120
Cowpea	All season	4-5 kg/acre	15 cm	30 cm	8	8-10 qtl/acre	100-120
Cluster bean	July	4-6 kg/acre	15 cm	45 cm	25	3-4 t/acre	100-120
Pigeon Pea	June-July	2-3 kg/acre	30 cm	60-90 cm	10-15	10-15 qtl/acre	100-120
Onion seed production	Nov	600-1200 g/acre	60 cm	120 cm	11	10-12 qtl/acre	120-130
Onion	All season	1000kg bulb/acre	30 cm	45 cm	-	4-5 qtl/acre	90-110

ཀྵ

VEGETABLE CROP PEST AND LIFECYCLE:

Crop	Common Name	Damaging Stage	Egg laying
Potato	Tuber Moth	Larva	Uncovered potato tuber
	Cut worm	Larva	Soil
	Aphids	Nymph	Upper surface of leaf
	Mite	Adult	Undersurface of leaf
	Cyst Nematode	J_2 and J_3	Tuber
Tomato	Root knot nematode	J_2 and J_3	Root
	Fruit borer	Larva	Leaf
	Whitefly	Nymph & Adult	Under surface of leaf
	Serpentine leaf minor	Larva	Leaf tissue
Radish	Mustard saw fly	Larva	
	Painted bug	Nymph & Adult	Leaf surface
Okra	Fruit & shoot borer	Larva	Fruit & shoot

	Leaf hopper	Nymph & Adult	Under surface of leaf
	Blister beetle	Grub & Adult	Soil
	Nematode	J_2 and J_3	Root
	Whitefly	Nymph & Adult	Under surface of leaf
Garlic & Onion	Thrips	Adult	Leaf tissue
	Mite	Adult & immature stage	Under surface of leaf
	Onion fly	Grab	On fruit
	Bulb nematode	J_2 and J_3	Bulb
French bean	Stem fly	Grab	Stem
Cucurbits	Red pumpkin beetle	Beetle, Nymph	Leaf surface
	Fruit fly	Larva & grab	Inside fruit
	Thrips	Adult	Leaf tissue
Chili	Thrips	Adult	Leaf tissue
	Whitefly	Nymph & Adult	Under surface of leaf
Cole crops	Diamond black moth	Larva	Leaves
	Stem borer	Larva & grab	Stem
	Head borer	Larva & grab	Head
Brinjal	Fruit & shoot borer	Larva	Fruit petiole
	Stem borer	Grab	Soil
	Ash weevil	Nymph & Adult	Leaves
	Epilachana (Hadda) beetle	Grab & Adult	Leaves
	Root knot nematode	J_2 and J_3	Root
Sweet Potato	Sweet potato weevil	Nymph & Adult	Soil
Turmeric & Ginger	Rhizome fly	Grab	Plant part and soil

Vegetable Crop Pest

A pest is any species of animal or pathogenic agent that injurious to plant or plant product. A pest is affect plant or plant part by eating or damaging. In this chapter we will learn different pest of vegetables and lifecycle of pest.

Tomato:

1.Pest : Fruit Borer (*Helicoverpa armigera)*

Life cycle: Egg- Larva- Pupa- Adult

Control measure(Dose ml/15 lit of water): Novaluton 10 % EC @10ml, Neem oil 10,000 ppm @ 15ml, Flubendamide 20 WG @ 7.5gm, Emamectin Benzoate 5% SG @ 10ml, *Bacillus thuringiensis* 30 gm, HNPV 1.5 x 10^{12} POBs/ha, Trap Crop : Merigold

2.Pest : Serpentine leaf minor *(Liriomyza trifolii)*

Life cycle: Larva-Pupa-Adult

Control measure(Dose ml/15 lit of water): Deltamethrin 2.8% EC @ 15ml, Neem oil 10,000 ppm @ 15ml

3.Pest : Tuta Absoluta (Pinworm)

Life cycle: Larva-Pupa-Adult

Control measure(Dose ml/15 lit of water): Deltamethrin 2.8% EC @ 15ml, Neem oil 10,000 ppm @ 15ml

4.Pest: Leaf eating caterpillar (*Spodoptera Letura)*

Life cycle: Egg-Larva-Adult

Control measure(Dose ml/15 lit of water): Cloropyriphos 20 EC @1 lit/acre, Flubendamide 20 WG @ 7.5gm, SNPV @1.5 x 10^{12} POBs/ha

5.Pest : White Fly (*Bemisia tabaci)*

Life cycle: Egg- Nymph- Adult

Control measure(Dose ml/15 lit of water): Thiomithoxam 25% WG @7gm, Imidacloprid 17.8 % SL @12ml, Dimethoate 30% EC @ 15ml

6.Pest : Thrips (*Thrips tabaci, F. rankliniella)*

Life cycle: Egg-Nymph- Adult

Control measure(Dose ml/15 lit of water): Spinosad 45% SC @5-7ml, Spinetoram 11.7% SC @ 15-20 ml

7.Pest : Mealy Bug (*Ferrisia virgata)*

Life cycle: Crawler – Adult

Control measure(Dose ml/15 lit of water): Thiomithoxam 25% WG @7gm, Imidacloprid 17.8 % SL @12ml, Profenophos 50 EC @30ml

8.Pest : Red Spider Mite (*Tetranychus spp.)*

Life cycle: Crawler – Adult

Control measure(Dose ml/15 lit of water): Profenophos 50 EC @30ml

Brinjal:

1. Shoot and Fruit Border (*Leucinodes orbonalis)*

Life cycle: Egg- Larva- Pupa- Adult

Control measure(Dose ml/15 lit of water): Novaluton 10 % EC @10ml, Neem oil 10,000 ppm @ 15ml, Flubendamide 20 WG @ 7.5gm, Emamectin

Benzoate 5% SG @ 10ml, *Bacillus thuringiensis* 30 gm, HNPV 1.5 x 10^{12} POBs/ ha, Trap Crop : Merigold

2. Stem Borer(*Euzophera perticella)*

Life cycle: Egg-Larva-Adult

Control measure(Dose ml/15 lit of water): Collect and destroy the damaged and dead plants, Flubendamide 20 WG @ 7.5gm, Emamectin Benzoate 5% SG @ 10ml

3. Hadda/ Spotted Beetle (*H.vigintioito punctata)*

Life cycle: Egg-Grub-Pupa-Adult

Control measure(Dose ml/15 lit of water): Thiomithoxam 25% WG @7gm, Imidacloprid 17.8 % SL @12ml

4. Ash Weevils (*Myllocerus subfasciatus)*

Life cycle: Grub- Pupa- Adult

Control measure(Dose ml/15 lit of water): Thiomithoxam 25% WG @7gm, Imidacloprid 17.8 % SL @12ml, Carbofuran 3 G @15 kg/ha

5. Brown Leaf Hopper (*Cestius phycitis)*

Life cycle: Egg-Larva-Adult

Control measure(Dose ml/15 lit of water): Dimethoate 0.3% @10 ml, Flubendamide 20 WG @ 7.5gm

6. Lace Wing Bug (*Urentius hystricellus)*

Life cycle: Egg-Nymph-Adult

Control measure(Dose ml/15 lit of water): Thiomithoxam 25% WG @7gm, Carbofuran 3 G @15 kg/ha

Chilli

1. Thrips (*Scirtothrips dorsalis)*

Life cycle: Nymph-Adult

Control measure(Dose ml/15 lit of water): Inter crop with Agathi, Spinosad 45% SC @5-7ml, Spinetoram 11.7% SC @ 15-20 ml

2. Green Peach Aphid (*Myzus persicae)*

Life cycle: Nymph- Adult

Control measure(Dose ml/15 lit of water): Thiomithoxam 25% WG @7gm, Imidacloprid 17.8 % SL @12ml, Quinalphos 25 % EC @ 10 ml

3. Tobacco cutworm (*Spodoptera litura)*

Life cycle: Egg-Larva-Adult

Control measure(Dose ml/15 lit of water): Flubendamide 20 WG @ 7.5gm, Emamectin Benzoate 5% SG @ 10ml, Novaluton 10 % EC @10ml

4. Gram Caterpiller (*Helicoverpa armigera*)

Life cycle: Egg-Larva-Pupa- Adult

Control measure(Dose ml/15 lit of water): Flubendamide 20 WG @ 7.5gm, Emamectin Benzoate 5% SG @ 10ml, Novaluton 10 % EC @10ml, Indoxacarb 14.5% SC @10 ml

5. Yellow Mite (*Polyphagotarsonemus latus*)

Life cycle: Egg- Nymph- Adult

Control measure(Dose ml/15 lit of water): Diafenthiuron 50 % WP @12 gm, Propergite 57% SC @35 ml,

Profenofos 50 % EC @ 25ml

Okra

1. Shoot and Fruit border(*Earias vitelli Helicoverpa armigera*)

Life cycle: Egg-Larva-Pupa-Adult

Control measure(Dose ml/15 lit of water): Novaluton 10 % EC @10ml, Neem oil 10,000 ppm @ 15ml, Flubendamide 20 WG @ 7.5gm, Emamectin Benzoate 5% SG @ 10ml, *Bacillus thuringiensis*30 gm, HNPV 1.5x1012 POB/ha

2. Shoot Weevil (*Alcidodes affaber*)

Life cycle: Grub- Adult

Control measure(Dose ml/15 lit of water): Carbofuran 3 G at 30 kg/ ha, Thiomithoxam 25% WG @7gm

3. Stem Weevil (*Pempherulus affinis*)

Life cycle: Grub-Adult

Control measure(Dose ml/15 lit of water): Carbofuran 3 G at 30 kg/ ha , Thiomithoxam 25% WG @7gm

4. Leaf Roller (*Sylepta derogata*)

Life cycle: Larva – Adult

Control measure(Dose ml/15 lit of water): Collect and destroy rolled leaves, Carbaryl 50 WP@ 30 ml

5. Semilooper (*Anomis flava*)

Life cycle: Egg-Larva-Adult

Control measure(Dose ml/15 lit of water): Novaluton 10 % EC @10ml, Neem oil 10,000 ppm @ 15ml, Flubendamide 20 WG @ 7.5gm

6. Whitefly (*Bemisia tabaci*)

Life cycle: Egg- Nymph- Adult

Control measure(Dose ml/15 lit of water): Thiomithoxam 25% WG @7gm, Imidacloprid 17.8 % SL @12ml

Dimethoate 30% EC @ 15ml

7. Jassid (*Amrasca devastans*)

Life cycle: Egg- Nymph- Adult

Control measure(Dose ml/15 lit of water): Thiomithoxam 25% WG @7gm, Imidacloprid 17.8 % SL @12ml, Quinalphos 25 % EC @ 10 ml

8. Aphid (*Aphis gossypii*)

Life cycle: Egg- Nymph- Adult

Control measure(Dose ml/15 lit of water): Thiomithoxam 25% WG @7gm, Imidacloprid 17.8 % SL @12ml, Quinalphos 25 % EC @ 10 ml

9. Red cotton bug (*Dysdercus cingulatus*)

Life cycle: Nymph- Adult

Control measure(Dose ml/15 lit of water): Diafenthiuron 50 % WP @12 gm, Propergite 57% SC @35 ml, Thiomithoxam 25% WG @7gm

Onion/Garlic/Leek

1. Thrips (*Thrips tabaci*)

Life cycle: Nymph-Adult

Control measure(Dose ml/15 lit of water): Spinosad 45% SC @5-7ml, Spinetoram 11.7% SC @ 15-20 ml

2. Onion maggot (*Hylemya antiqua*)

Life cycle: Egg-Larva-Maggot-Adult

Control measure(Dose ml/15 lit of water): Profenophos 40% + Cypermethrin 4% EC @30 ml, Flubendamide 20 WG @ 7.5gm

Cucurbits

1. Fruit Flies (*Bactrocera cucurbitae*)

Life cycle: Egg- Larva- Pupa

Control measure(Dose ml/15 lit of water): Use traps

2. Pumpkin beetles/ Red Beetles (*Aulacophora foveicollis*)

Life cycle: Grub- Adult

Control measure(Dose ml/15 lit of water): Thiomithoxam 25% WG @7gm, Imidacloprid 17.8 % SL @12ml, Malathion 50 EC @ 20 ml

3. Stem Borer (*Melittia eurytion*)

Life cycle: Larva- Pupa- Adult

Control measure(Dose ml/15 lit of water): Novaluton 10 % EC @10ml, Neem oil 10,000 ppm @ 15ml, Flubendamide 20 WG @ 7.5gm, Emamectin

Benzoate 5% SG @ 10ml

4. Snake Gourd Semilooper (*Plusia peponis*)

Life cycle: Egg- Larva- Pupa- Adult

Control measure(Dose ml/15 lit of water): Novaluton 10 % EC @10ml, Neem oil 10,000 ppm @ 15ml

5. Pumpkin Caterpiller (*Diaphania indica*)

Life cycle: Egg- Larva- Pupa- Adult

Control measure(Dose ml/15 lit of water): Cloropyriphos 20 EC @1 lit/ acre, Flubendamide 20 WG @ 7.5gm

6. Bottler Gourd Plume Moth (*Sphenarches caffer*)

Life cycle: Egg- Larva- Pupa- Adult

Control measure(Dose ml/15 lit of water): Dimethoate 30% EC @ 15ml, Flubendamide 20 WG @ 7.5gm

7. Leaf Minor (*Liriomyza trifolii*)

Life cycle: Larva-Pupa- Adult

Control measure(Dose ml/15 lit of water): Deltamethrin 2.8% EC @ 15ml, Neem oil 10,000 ppm @ 15ml

ꕥ

Cole crops

1. Diamond Black Moth (DBM) (*Plutella xylostella*)

Life cycle: Egg- Larva- Pupa- Adult

Control measure(Dose ml/15 lit of water): Pheromone traps @12/ha, Crop rotation with cucurbits, beans, peas, tomato and melon, *Bacillus thuringiensis var kurstaki* 2g/lit, Neem oil 10,000 ppm @ 15ml, Deltamethrin 2.8 EC @ 20 ml

2. Cabbage Borer (*Hellula undalis*)

Life cycle: Egg-Larva-Pupa-Adult

Control measure(Dose ml/15 lit of water): Flubendamide 20 WG @ 7.5gm, Emamectin Benzoate 5% SG @ 10ml, *Bacillus thuringiensis*30 gm, Cartap Hydrocloride @7gm

3. Leaf Webber (*Crocidolomia binotalis*)

Life cycle: Egg-Larva-Pupa-Adult

Control measure(Dose ml/15 lit of water): Remove and destroy the webbed leaves with caterpillars within

Set up light traps@1/ha, Deltamethrin 2.8 EC @ 20 ml

4. Cabbage Green Semilooper (*Trichoplusia ni*)

Life cycle: Egg-Larva-Adult

Control measure(Dose ml/15 lit of water): Novaluton 10 % EC @10ml, Neem oil 10,000 ppm @ 15ml, Flubendamide 20 WG @ 7.5gm

5. Cabbage Butterfly (*Pieris brassicae*)

Life cycle: Larva-Pupa-Adult

Control measure(Dose ml/15 lit of water): Collect and destroy caterpillars in the early stage of attack

Conserve parasitoids like *Cotesia glomeratus*, Quinalphos 25 % EC @ 10 ml

6. Tobbaco Caterpiller (*podoptera litura*)

Life cycle: Egg-Larva-Adult

Control measure(Dose ml/15 lit of water): Flubendamide 20 WG @ 7.5gm, Emamectin Benzoate 5% SG @ 10ml, Novaluton 10 % EC @10ml, SNPV @1.5 x 10^{12} POBs/ha

7. Cabbage Aphid (*Brevicoryne brassicae*)

Life cycle: Nymph- Adult

Control measure(Dose ml/15 lit of water): Thiomithoxam 25% WG @7gm, Imidacloprid 17.8 % SL @12ml, Quinalphos 25 % EC @ 10 ml

8. Mustard Aphid (*Lipaphis erysimi*)

Life cycle: Nymph- Adult

Control measure(Dose ml/15 lit of water): Thiomithoxam 25% WG @7gm, Imidacloprid 17.8 % SL @12ml, Quinalphos 25 % EC @ 10 ml

Potato

1. Cutworm (*Agrotis ipsilon*)

Life cycle: Egg-Larva-Pupa-Adult

Control measure(Dose ml/15 lit of water): Flubendamide 20 WG @ 7.5gm, Emamectin Benzoate 5% SG @ 10ml, Novaluton 10 % EC @10ml

2. Potato Tuber Moth (*Phthorimaea operculella*)

Life cycle: Egg-Larva-Pupa-Adult

Control measure(Dose ml/15 lit of water): Collect and destroy all the infested tubers from the field, Do not leave the harvested tubers in the field overnight, Do earthing up at 60 days after planting to avoid female moths laying eggs on the exposed tubers, *Bacillus thuringiensis var kurstaki* 2g/lit, Neem oil 10,000 ppm @ 15ml, Deltamethrin 2.8 EC @ 20 ml

3. White Grub (*Holotrichia sp.*)

Life cycle: Larva-Adult

Control measure(Dose ml/15 lit of water): Carbofuran 3 G at 30 kg/ ha , Thiomithoxam 25% WG @7gm

4. Tobacco Caterpiller (*Spodoptera litura)*

Control measure(Dose ml/15 lit of water): Flubendamide 20 WG @ 7.5gm, Emamectin Benzoate 5% SG @ 10ml, Novaluton 10 % EC @10ml, SNPV @1.5 x 10^{12} POBs/ha

5. Green Leaf Hopper (*Empoasca kerri)*

Life cycle: Egg-Nymph-Adult

Control measure(Dose ml/15 lit of water): Dimethoate 30% EC @ 15ml, Flubendamide 20 WG @ 7.5gm

6. Green Peach Aphid (*Myzus persicae)*

Life cycle: Nymph- Adult

Control measure(Dose ml/15 lit of water): Thiomithoxam 25% WG @7gm, Imidacloprid 17.8 % SL @12ml, Quinalphos 25 % EC @ 10 ml

7. Whitefly (*Bemisia tabaci)*

Life cycle: Egg- Nymph- Adult

Control measure(Dose ml/15 lit of water): Thiomithoxam 25% WG @7gm, Imidacloprid 17.8 % SL @12ml, Dimethoate 30% EC @ 15ml

Sweet Potato

1. Weevil (*Cylas formicarius)*

Life cycle: Egg-Larva-Pupa-Adult

Control measure(Dose ml/15 lit of water): Set the trap at 5 m apart at 4 PM, collect and destroy adult weevils at 6 AM next day, Rake up the soil and earth up at 50 days after planting, Crop rotation with rice between two sweet potato, Carbofuran 3 G @30 kg/ ha , Thiomithoxam 25% WG @7gm

2. Tortoise Beetle (*Cassida circumdata)*

Life cycle: Grub-Pupa-Adult

Control measure(Dose ml/15 lit of water): Use yellow sticky trap @12/ha, Carbofuran 3G @ 30 kg/ ha, Thiomithoxam 25% WG @7gm

Vegetable Crop Disease

When plant is continuously disturbed by some organisms results in abnormal physiological process that disrupt plant structure, growth, function etc. is called disease. These organisms may be fungi, bacteria or virus. In plant we can see proper sign and symptoms of particular disease.

Tomato

1. Damping off (*Pythium aphanidermatum)*

Fungal

Control Measure (Dose ml/15 lit of water): Copper oxychloride 45 gm, Carbendazim 50 % 35 gm, *Trichoderma viride,* Mancozeb 35 gm

2. Early blight (*Alternaria solani)*

Fungal

Control Measure (Dose ml/15 lit of water): Mancozeb 35 gm, Crop rotation helps to minimize the disease

3. Fusarium Wilt (*Fusarium oxysporum f. sp. lycopersici)*

Fungal

Control Measure (Dose ml/15 lit of water): Copper oxychloride 45 gm, , Carbendazim 50 % 35 gm, Hexaconazole 5% SC 30 ml, Crop rotation with a non-host crop such as cereals

4. Saptoria Leaf Spot (*Septoria lycopersici)*

Fungal

Control Measure (Dose ml/15 lit of water): Copper oxychloride 45 gm, Carbendazim 50 % 35 gm

5. Becterial Wilt (*Burkholderia solanacearum)*

Bacteria

Control Measure (Dose ml/15 lit of water): Copper oxychloride 45 gm + Streptomycin 2 gm

6. Bacterial Leaf Spot (*Xanthomonas campestris pv. vesicatoria)*

Bacteria

Control Measure (Dose ml/15 lit of water): Copper oxychloride 45 gm + Streptomycin 2 gm, Seed treatment with mercuric chloride

7. Tomato Mosaic Virus

Transmitted by: Aphid and also Spread by contact with clothes, hand of working labor, touching of infected plants with healthy ones

Control Measure (Dose ml/15 lit of water): Thiomithoxam 25% WG @7gm, Imidacloprid 17.8 % SL @12ml

Soaking of the seeds in a solution of Trisodium Phosphate (90 g/litre of water) a day before sowing, Crop rotation with crops other than tobacco, potato, chilli, capsicum, brinjal

8. Tomato Leaf Curl Virus

Transmitted by: Whitefly

Control Measure (Dose ml/15 lit of water): Keep yellow sticky traps @ 12/ha, Thiomithoxam 25% WG @7gm, Imidacloprid 17.8 % SL @12ml, Dimethoate 30% EC @ 15ml

9. Tomato Spotted Wilt Disease

Transmitted by: Thrips

Control Measure (Dose ml/15 lit of water): Spinosad 45% SC @5-7ml, Spinetoram 11.7% SC @ 15-20 ml

Brinjal

1. Bacterial wilt (*Pseudomonas solanacearum*)

Bacteria

Control Measure (Dose ml/15 lit of water): Copper oxychloride 45 gm + Streptomycin 2 gm, Bordeaux Mixture 2 %

2. Cercospora Leaf Spot (*Cercospora solani -melongenae*)

Fungal

Control Measure (Dose ml/15 lit of water): Copper oxychloride 45 gm + Streptomycin 2 gm, Bordeaux Mixture 2 %

3. Alternaria Leaf Spot (*Alternaria melongenae*)

Bacteria

Control Measure (Dose ml/15 lit of water): Carbendezom 50% 35 gm, Copper oxychloride 45 gm + Streptomycin 2 gm, Bordeaux Mixture 2 %

4. Damping off (*Pythium aphanidermatum*)

Fungal

Control Measure (Dose ml/15 lit of water): Copper oxychloride 45 gm, Carbendazim 50 % 35 gm, *Trichoderma viride,* Mancozeb 35 gm

5. Tobacco Mosaic Virus

Transmitted by: whitefly

Control Measure (Dose ml/15 lit of water): Keep yellow sticky traps @ 12/ha, Thiomithoxam 25% WG @7gm, Imidacloprid 17.8 % SL @12ml , Dimethoate 30% EC @ 15ml

6. Collar rot (*Sclerotium rolfsii*)

Fungal

Control Measure (Dose ml/15 lit of water): Copper oxychloride 45 gm, Carbendazim 50 % 35 gm, *Trichoderma viride,* Mancozeb 35 gm

Okra

1. Cercospora Leaf Spot (*Cercospora malayensis*)

Fungal

Control Measure (Dose ml/15 lit of water): Copper oxychloride 45 gm + Streptomycin 2 gm, Bordeaux Mixture 2 %

2. Fusarium Wilt (*Fusarium oxysporum f.sp. vasinfectum*)

Fungal

Control Measure (Dose ml/15 lit of water): Copper oxychloride 45 gm, Carbendazim 50 % 35 gm, Hexaconazole 5% SC 30 ml, Crop rotation with a non-host crop such as cereals

3. Powdery Mildew (*Erysiphe cichoracearum*)

Fungal

Control Measure (Dose ml/15 lit of water): Hexaconazole 5% SC 30 ml, Hexa 4% + Zineb 35 gm, Sulphur dusting

4. Yellow Vein Mosaic Virus

Transmitted by Whitefly

Control Measure (Dose ml/15 lit of water): Keep yellow sticky traps @ 12/ha, Thiomithoxam 25% WG , @7gm, Imidacloprid 17.8 % SL @12ml, Dimethoate 30% EC @ 15ml

Chilli

1. Dmping off (*Pythium aphanidermatum*)

Fungal

Control Measure (Dose ml/15 lit of water): Copper oxychloride 45 gm, Carbendazim 50 % 35 gm, *Trichoderma viride*, Mancozeb 35 gm

2. Fruit Rot/ Die back (*Colletotrichum capsici*)

Fungal

Control Measure (Dose ml/15 lit of water): Hexaconazole 5% SC 30 ml, Hexa 4% + Zineb 35 gm, Tebuconazole 10% + Sulphur 65 % WG 50 gm

3. Powdery Mildew (*Leveillula taurica*)

Fungal

Control Measure (Dose ml/15 lit of water): Hexaconazole 5% SC 30 ml, Hexa 4% + Zineb 35 gm, Sulphur dusting

4. Bacterial Leaf Spot (*Xanthomonas campestris pv. vesicatoria*)

Bacteria

Control Measure (Dose ml/15 lit of water): Copper oxychloride 45 gm + Streptomycin 2 gm, Hexaconazole 5% SC 30 ml, Bordeaux Mixture 2 %

5. Cercospora Leaf Spot (*Cercospora capsici*)

Fungal

Control Measure (Dose ml/15 lit of water): Copper oxychloride 45 gm + Streptomycin 2 gm, Bordeaux Mixture 2 %

6. Fusarium Wilt (*Fusarium oxysporum f.sp.capsici*)

Fungal

Control Measure (Dose ml/15 lit of water): Copper oxychloride 45 gm, Carbendazim 50 % 35 gm, Hexaconazole 5% SC 30 ml, Crop rotation with a non-host crop such as cereals

7. Leaf Curl Virus

Transmitted by Whitefly

Control Measure (Dose ml/15 lit of water): Keep yellow sticky traps @ 12/ha, Thiomithoxam 25% WG @7gm, Imidacloprid 17.8 % SL @12ml, Dimethoate 30% EC @ 15ml

Onion/Garlic

1. Basal Rot (*Fusarium oxysporum f.sp. cepae*)

Fungal (This disease can begin in the field and continue on in storage)

Control Measure (Dose ml/15 lit of water): Copper oxychloride 45 gm, Carbendazim 50 % 35 gm, Hexaconazole 5% SC 30 ml, Tebuconazole 25.9 WW

2. Downy Mildew (*Peronospora destructor*)

Fungal

Control Measure (Dose ml/15 lit of water): Copper oxychloride 45 gm, Carbendazim 50 % 35 gm, *Trichoderma viride*, Mancozeb 35 gm

3. Leaf Blight (Blast) (*Botrytis spp.*)

Fungal

Control Measure (Dose ml/15 lit of water): Carbendazim 50 % 35 gm, *Trichoderma viride*, Mancozeb 35 gm

4. Phythium Root rot (*Pythium aphanidermatum*)

Fungal

Control Measure (Dose ml/15 lit of water): Copper oxychloride 45 gm + Streptomycin 2 gm, Hexaconazole 5% SC 30 ml, Bordeaux Mixture 2 %

5. Smut (*Urocystis cepulae*)

Fungal

Control Measure (Dose ml/15 lit of water): Hexaconazole 5% SC 30 ml, Hexa 4% + Zineb 35 gm, Tebuconazole 10% + Sulphur 65 % WG 50 gm

6. White Rot (*Sclerotium cepivorum*)

Fungal

Control Measure (Dose ml/15 lit of water): Carbendazim 50 % 35 gm, Hexaconazole 5% SC 30 ml,

Tebuconazole 25.9 WW

7. Purple Blotch (*Alternaria porri*)

Fungal

Control Measure (Dose ml/15 lit of water): Chlorothalonil 0.2 %, Carbendazim 50 % 35 gm, Hexaconazole 5% SC 30 ml, Tebuconazole 25.9 WW

ꝏ

Beans

1. Anthracnose (*Colletotrichum lindemuthianum*)

Fungal

Control Measure (Dose ml/15 lit of water): Hexaconazole 5% SC 30 ml, Hexa 4% + Zineb 35 gm, Tebuconazole 10% + Sulphur 65 % WG 50 gm

2. Bean Root Rot (*Rhizoctonia solani, Pythium, Fusarium solani*)

Fungal

Control Measure (Dose ml/15 lit of water): Hexaconazole 5% SC 30 ml, Hexa 4% + Zineb 35 gm, Tebuconazole 10% + Sulphur 65 % WG 50 gm

3. Rust (*Uromyces appendiculaters*)

Fungal (The fungus survives the winter in the soil, on plant debris and even on poles used the previous year)

Control Measure (Dose ml/15 lit of water): Copper oxychloride 45 gm, Carbendazim 50 % 35 gm, Pyroclostrabin 5%+ Matiram 55% WG

4. Bacterial Blight (*Xanthomonas campestris pv phaseoli*)

Bacterial

Control Measure (Dose ml/15 lit of water): Copper oxychloride 45 gm + Streptomycin 2 gm, Bordeaux Mixture 2 %

5. Mosaic Virus

Aphid and Nutrient imbalance

Control Measure (Dose ml/15 lit of water): Thiomithoxam 25% WG @7gm, Imidacloprid 17.8 % SL @12ml

6. Powdery Mildew (*Erysiphe polygonii*)

Fungal

Control Measure (Dose ml/15 lit of water): Hexaconazole 5% SC 30 ml, Hexa 4% + Zineb 35 gm, Sulphur dusting

7. Cercospora Leaf Spot (*Cercospora sp.*)

Fungal

Control Measure (Dose ml/15 lit of water): Copper oxychloride 45 gm + Streptomycin 2 gm, Bordeaux Mixture 2 %

8. Watery Soft Rot (*Sclerotinia sclerotiorum*)

Fungal (Improve air circulation between plants and rows)

Control Measure (Dose ml/15 lit of water): Carbendazim 50% 35 gm, Mencozeb 35 gm

9. Angular Leaf Spot (*Phaeoisariopsis griseola)*

Fungal (Specially in French Bean)

Control Measure (Dose ml/15 lit of water): Carbendazim 50% 35 gm, Mencozeb 35 gm

10. Fusarium Wilt (*Fusarium oxysporum f.sp. pisi)*

Fungal (Found in Peas majority)

Control Measure (Dose ml/15 lit of water): Copper oxychloride 45 gm, Carbendazim 50 % 35 gm, Hexaconazole 5% SC 30 ml, Crop rotation with a non-host crop such as cereals

Gourds

1. Powdery Mildew (*Erysiphe cichoracearum)*

Fungal

Control Measure (Dose ml/15 lit of water): Hexaconazole 5% SC 30 ml, Hexa 4% + Zineb 35 gm

2. Downy Mildew (*Pseudoperonospora cubensis)*

Fungal

Control Measure (Dose ml/15 lit of water): Copper oxychloride 45 gm, Carbendazim 50 % 35 gm, Mancozeb 35 gm, Seed treatment with Apron SD 35 @ 2 g./kg

3. Mosaic

Transmitted by Aphid

Control Measure (Dose ml/15 lit of water): Thiomithoxam 25% WG @7gm, Imidacloprid 17.8 % SL @12ml, Flonicamid 50 WG @6 gm

Watermelon and Muskmelon

1. Gummy Stem Blight (*Mycosphaerella melonis*

Fungal

Control Measure (Dose ml/15 lit of water): Carbendazim 50 % 35 gm, Hexaconazole 5% SC 30 ml

2. Bacterial Wilt (Erwinia tracheiphila)

Bacteria

Control Measure (Dose ml/15 lit of water): Copper oxychloride 45 gm, Bordeaux Mixture 2 %

3. Fusarium Wilt (*Fusarium oxysporum f. sp. melonis*)

Fungal

Control Measure (Dose ml/15 lit of water): Copper oxychloride 45 gm, Carbendazim 50 % 35 gm, Hexaconazole 5% SC 30 ml, Crop rotation with a non-host crop such as cereals

4. Anthracnose (*Colletotrichum orbiculare*)

Fungal

Control Measure (Dose ml/15 lit of water): Copper oxychloride 45 gm, Carbendazim 50 % 35 gm

5. Powdery Mildew (*Erysiphe cichoracearum*)

Fungal

Control Measure (Dose ml/15 lit of water): Hexaconazole 5% SC 30 ml, Hexa 4% + Zineb 35 gm, Wettable sulphur @ 0.2%

6. Alternaria Blight (*Alternaria cucumerina*)

Fungal

Control Measure (Dose ml/15 lit of water): Copper oxychloride 45 gm, Tebuconazole 10% + Sulphur 65 % WG 50 gm, Mencozeb 35 gm

7. Downy Mildew (*Pseudoperonospora cubensis*)

Fungal

Control Measure (Dose ml/15 lit of water): Azoxystrobin 11% + Tebuconazole 18.3% SC @ 25ml, Carbendazim 50 % 35 gm

8. Angular Leaf Spot (*Pseudomonas lachrymans*)

Fungal

Control Measure (Dose ml/15 lit of water): Carbendazim 50% 35 gm, Mencozeb 35 gm

Cole Crops

1. Bacterial Blight (*Xanthomonas campestris pv.carotae*)

Bacteria

Control Measure (Dose ml/15 lit of water): Mainly found in Carrot, Copper oxychloride 45 gm, Bordeaux Mixture 2 %

2. *Bacterial Soft Rot (Erwinia carotovora sp. Carotovora)*

Bacteria

Control Measure (Dose ml/15 lit of water): Mainly found in Carrot, Dipping in a solution of 1:500 of sodium hypochlorite before storage

3. Cercospora Leaf Spot (*Cercospora carotae)*

Fungal

Control Measure (Dose ml/15 lit of water): Mainly found in Carrot, Copper oxychloride 45 gm + , Streptomycin 2 gm, Bordeaux Mixture 2 %

4. Sclerotinia Rot/ White Mold (*Sclerotinia sclerotiorum)*

Fungal

Control Measure (Dose ml/15 lit of water): Mainly found in Carrot, Frequent inspection in storage, low temperatures, aeration and washing in a final water of 2-5 % diluted bleach solution

5. Alternaria Blight (*Alternaria raphani)*

Fungal

Control Measure (Dose ml/15 lit of water): Carbendazim 50% 35 gm, Mencozeb 35 gm

6. White Rust(*Albugo candida)*

Fungal

Control Measure (Dose ml/15 lit of water): Mainly found in Radish, Copper oxychloride 45 gm, Carbendazim 50 % 35 gm

Cabbage & Cauliflower

1. Black Leg (*Phoma lingam)*

Fungal

Control Measure (Dose ml/15 lit of water): Copper oxychloride 45 gm, Carbendazim 50 % 35 gm, *Trichoderma viride*

2. Downy Mildew (Peronospora parasitica)

Fungal

Control Measure (Dose ml/15 lit of water): Metalaxyl, Hexaconazole 5% SC 30 ml, Tebuconazole 18.3% SC @ 25ml

3. Root Rot/ Wire Stem (*Rhizoctonia solani)*

Fungal

Control Measure (Dose ml/15 lit of water): Copper oxychloride 45 gm + Streptomycin 2 gm, Bordeaux Mixture 2 %

4. Black Spot (*Alternaria sp.)*

Fungal

Control Measure (Dose ml/15 lit of water): Carbendazim 50 % 35 gm, Pyroclostrabin 5%+ Matiram 55% WG

5. Clubroot (*Plasmodiophora brassicae*)

Fungal

Control Measure (Dose ml/15 lit of water): Soil fumigation with Methly bromide 1kg/10m, Soil drenching with Copper oxychloride

6. Powdery Mildew (*Erysiphe polygoni*)

Fungal

Control Measure (Dose ml/15 lit of water): Hexaconazole 5% SC 30 ml, Hexa 4% + Zineb 35 gm, Wettable sulphur @ 0.2%

7. Damping Off (*Pythium debaryanum*)

Fungal

Control Measure (Dose ml/15 lit of water): Copper oxychloride 45 gm, Soil drenching with Carbendazim 50 % 35 gm, *Trichoderma viride,* Mancozeb 35 gm

8. Black Rot (*Xanthomonas campestris pv. campestris*)

Bacteria

Control Measure (Dose ml/15 lit of water): yellow 'V' shaped spots arising along the margin which extend in the direction of the midrib, Copper oxychloride 45 gm, Bordeaux Mixture 2 %

Potato

1. Late Blight (*Phytopthora infestans*)

Fungal

Control Measure (Dose ml/15 lit of water): The infected tubers and the infected soil may serve as a source of primary infection, Hexaconazole 5% SC 30 ml, Tebuconazole 25.9 WW, Pyroclostrabin 5%+ Matiram 55% WG

2. Early Blight (Alternaria solani)

Bacteria

Control Measure (Dose ml/15 lit of water): Copper oxychloride 45 gm, Carbendazim 50 % 35 gm, *Trichoderma viride,* Mancozeb 35 gm

3. Post-Harvest Tuber rots (*Sclerotium rolfsii*)

Fungal

Control Measure (Dose ml/15 lit of water): Treating seeds with mercury compounds after harvest reduces tuber rot, The disease is low in the variety Kufri Sindhuri

4. Black Scurf (*Rhizoctonia solani*)

Fungal

Control Measure (Dose ml/15 lit of water): Copper oxychloride 45 gm + Streptomycin 2 gm, Bordeaux Mixture 2 %

5. Common Scab/ Corkey Scab (*Streptomyces scabies*)

Bacterial

Control Measure (Dose ml/15 lit of water): Copper oxychloride 45 gm + Streptomycin 2 gm, Azoxystrobin 11% + Tebuconazole 18.3% SC @ 25 ml

6. Brown Rot/ Bangle Blight (*Ralstonia solanacearum*)

Bacterial

Control Measure (Dose ml/15 lit of water): Crop rotation of wheat along with potato, Copper oxychloride 45 gm + Streptomycin 2 gm

7. Bacterial Soft Rot (*Erwinia carotovora subsp caratovora*)

Bacterial

Control Measure (Dose ml/15 lit of water): Copper oxychloride 45 gm + Streptomycin 2 gm, Bordeaux Mixture 2 %

Sweet Potato

1. Black Rot(*Ceratocystis fimbriata*)

Fungal

Control Measure (Dose ml/15 lit of water): Hexaconazole 5% SC 30 ml, Tebuconazole 25.9 WW

2. *Rhizophus Soft Rot (Rhizopus stolonifer)*

Fungal

Control Measure (Dose ml/15 lit of water): Copper oxychloride 45 gm, Carbendazim 50 % 35 gm, *Trichoderma viride*, Mancozeb 35 gm

3. Bacterial Soft Rot (*Erwinia chrysanthemi*)

Bacterial

Control Measure (Dose ml/15 lit of water): Copper oxychloride 45 gm + Streptomycin 2 gm, Bordeaux Mixture 2 %

4. Scurf (*Monilochaetes infuscans*)

Fungal

Control Measure (Dose ml/15 lit of water): Copper oxychloride 45 gm + Streptomycin 2 gm, Azoxystrobin 11% + Tebuconazole 18.3% SC @ 25 ml

5. Charcoal Rot (*Macrophomina phaseolina*)

Fungal

Control Measure (Dose ml/15 lit of water): Hexaconazole 5% SC 30 ml, Tebuconazole 25.9 WW

III

Fruit Crop Capsule

Generally, fruit is fleshy or dry ripened ovary surrounding the seed of a plant. Scientifically fruit is fleshy edible part of a perennial plant associated with development of the flower. Fruits are rich in nutrients and vitamins including wide range of health-boosting antioxidants also. The major difference between fruits and vegetable is fruits are eaten without cooking while vegetables are generally cooked before eat.

Crop	Sowing Time	Spacing(m)	Plant /acre	Flowering Time	Harvesting Time	First yield start after	Yield/ plant	Yield/acre
Mango	June-July	10*10 HDP 10*5	40	Dec.-Jan	April-May	5 yr	150 kg	4-6 t
Banana	May-July	1.8*1.8	1234	Nov.-Jan	March-May	12 month	30-45 kg	25-26t
Papaya	July-August, Feb-March	2.5*2.5	640	Aug-Nov	Feb-March	10 month	50-60kg	40 t
Pomegranate	June-July	6*6	110	January-February(ambe bahar) June July (mrig bahar) September-October (hasta bahar). For GUJRAT	June to September December to February March to April	3 - 4 yr	150-200 fruits	8 t
Guava	June-July	6*6	110	January-February(ambe bahar) June July (mrig bahar) For GUJRAT September-October (hasta bahar)	June to September December to February March to April	5 yr	150kg	4-6t
Sapota	June-July	10*10 HDP 10*5	40	Oct - Nov Feb-march	Jan - Feb May - June	5 yr	100-125 kg	5t
Ber	June-July	6*6	110	Aug-sep	Dec-Jan	3-4 yr	125-130kg	3-4t

Aonla	June-July	8*8	63	July-august	July-Aug	3 yr	125-130kg	6-7t
Coconut	June-July	Hybrid :- 7.5*7.5 Dwarf : 6*6	110	Every Month	6-7 month for tender nut	6-7 month for tender nut	70-80 fruits	7000-8000 fruits
Lemon	June-July	4.5*4.5	198	January-February(ambe bahar) May-June (mrig bahar) October (hasta bahar) For Gujrat	July to September Oct-Jan Feb-may	3-4 yr	40-70kg	8-9t
Clustard Apple	June-July	6*6	110	July-august	Nov-Dec	3-4 yr	50-100 fruits	3-4t

ꙮ

Fruit Crop Pest

Mango

1. Stem Borer (*Batocera rufomaculata*)

Life cycle: Grub-Adult

Control measure(Dose ml/15 lit of water): Swab Coal tar + Kerosene @ 1:2 or Carbaryl 50 WP 20 g / l (basal portion of the trunk - 3 feet height) after scraping the loose bark to prevent oviposition by adult b**eetles, Carbofuran 3 G @30 kg/ ha**

2. Bark Borer (*Indarbela tetraonis*)

Life cycle: Egg-Larva-Adult

Control measure(Dose ml/15 lit of water): Apply Copper Oxychloride paste on trunk, Carbofuran 3 G @30 kg/ ha

3. Shoot Borer (*Clumetia transversa*)

Life cycle: Larva-Adult

Control measure(Dose ml/15 lit of water): Collect and destroy the infested plant parts, Summer ploughing to expose the pupae

4. Mango Hopper (*Idioscopus niveoparsus)*

Life cycle: Egg-Nymph-Adult

Control measure(Dose ml/15 lit of water): Dimethoate 30% EC @ 15ml, Flubendamide 20 WG @ 7.5gm, Acephate 75 SP @ 15 gm

5. Aphid (*Toxoptera odinae)*

Life cycle: Egg-Nymph-Adult

Control measure(Dose ml/15 lit of water): Thiomithoxam 25% WG @7gm, Imidacloprid 17.8 % SL @12ml

6. Loopers (*Thalassodes quadraria)*

Life cycle: Egg-Nymph-Adult

Control measure(Dose ml/15 lit of water): Use light trap 1/ha to attract and kill the adults, Thiomithoxam 25% WG @7gm

7. Fruit Fly (*Bactrocera (Dacus) dorsalis)*

Life cycle: Egg-Larva-Adult

Control measure(Dose ml/15 lit of water): Dimethoate 30% EC @ 15ml, Flubendamide 20 WG @ 7.5gm

8. Mango Nut Weevil (*Sternochaetus mangiferae)*

Life cycle: Grub-Adult

Control measure(Dose ml/15 lit of water): Acephate 75 SP @ 15 gm, Thiamethoxam 12.6% + Lambdacyhalothrin 9.5% ZC @ 10ml

9. Shoot Webber (*Orthaga exvinacea)*

Life cycle: Egg-Larva-Adult

Control measure(Dose ml/15 lit of water): Profenophos 50 EC @30ml, Thiamethoxam 12.6% + Lambdacyhalothrin 9.5% ZC @ 10ml

10. Leaf Gall Midge

Life cycle: Maggots-Adult

Control measure(Dose ml/15 lit of water): Dimethoate 30% EC @ 15ml

11. Hairy Catterpiller (*Euproctis fraterna)*

Life cycle: Larva-Grub

Control measure(Dose ml/15 lit of water): Profenophos 50 EC @30ml, Thiomithoxam 25% WG @7gm

Use burning torch to kill the congregating larvae

12. Scale

Life cycle: Egg- Nymph-Adult

Control measure(Dose ml/15 lit of water): Pruning of infested branches and burning, Thiamethoxam 12.6% + Lambdacyhalothrin 9.5% ZC @ 10ml

13. Gaint Mealybug (*Drosicha mangiferae)*

Life cycle: Release of Australian ladybird beetle

Control measure(Dose ml/15 lit of water): Carbofuran 3 G @30 kg/ ha

14 Red Ant (*Oecophylla smaradina*)

Sapota

1. Bud Worm (*Anarsia epotias*)

Life cycle: Larva-Adult

Control measure(Dose ml/15 lit of water): Neem oil 10,000 ppm @ 15ml

2. Fruit Fly (*Bactrocera (Dacus) dorsalis*)

Life cycle: Egg-Larva-Pupa-Adult

Control measure(Dose ml/15 lit of water): Collect fallen infested fruits and dispose them by dumping in a pit and covering with soil, Provide summer ploughing to expose the pupa, Dimethoate 30% EC @ 15ml, Flubendamide 20 WG @ 7.5gm

3. Stem borer (*Plocaederus ferrugineus*)

Control measure(Dose ml/15 lit of water): Collect and destroy the damaged and dead plants, Flubendamide 20 WG @ 7.5gm, Emamectin Benzoate 5% SG @ 10ml, Carbofuran 3 G @30 kg/ ha

4. Leaf Webber (*Nephopteyrx eugraphella*)

Life cycle: Egg-Larva-Adult

Control measure(Dose ml/15 lit of water): Remove and destroy the webbed leaves with caterpillars within, Set up light traps@1/ha, Deltamethrin 2.8 EC @ 20 ml

5. Hairy Caterpiller (*Metanastria hytaca*)

Life cycle: Larva-Pupa-Adult

Control measure(Dose ml/15 lit of water): Profenophos 50 EC @30ml, Thiomithoxam 25% WG @7gm, Use burning torch to kill the congregating larvae

6. Striped Mealy Bug (*Ferrisia virgate*)

Life cycle: Egg-Larva-Adult

Control measure(Dose ml/15 lit of water): Profenophos 50 EC @30ml

7. Green Scale (*Coccus viridis*)

Life cycle: Egg-Nymph-Adult

Control measure(Dose ml/15 lit of water): Pruning of infested branches and burning, Thiamethoxam 12.6% + Lambdacyhalothrin 9.5% ZC @ 10ml

Guava

1. Fruit Borer (*Congethes punctiferalis*)

Life cycle: Egg-Larva-Pupa-Adult

Control measure(Dose ml/15 lit of water): Novaluton 10 % EC @10ml, Neem oil 10,000 ppm @ 15ml, Flubendamide 20 WG @ 7.5gm, Emamectin Benzoate 5% SG @ 10ml, *Bacillus thuringiensis* 30 gm, HNPV 1.5 x 10^{12} POBs/ha, Trap Crop : Merigold

2. Fruit Fly (*Bactrocera diversus*)

Life cycle: Egg-Larva-Adult

Control measure(Dose ml/15 lit of water): Dimethoate 30% EC @ 15ml, Flubendamide 20 WG @ 7.5gm

3. Bark Eating Caterpiller (*Indarbella sp.*)

Life cycle: Egg-Larva- Adult

Control measure(Dose ml/15 lit of water): Profenophos 50 EC @30ml, Thiomithoxam 25% WG @7gm, Use burning torch to kill the congregating larvae

4. Tea Mosquito Bug (*Helopeltis antonii*)

Life cycle: Egg-Nymph-Adult

Control measure(Dose ml/15 lit of water): Collect and destroy the damaged plant parts, Thiomithoxam 25% WG @7gm, Profenophos 50 EC @30ml

5. Green Scale (*Coccus viridis*)

Life cycle: Egg-Nymph-Adult

Control measure(Dose ml/15 lit of water): Pruning of infested branches and burning, Thiamethoxam 12.6% + Lambdacyhalothrin 9.5% ZC @ 10ml

6. Tailed Mealy Bug (*Ferrisa virgata*)

Life cycle: Egg-Nymph-Adult

Control measure(Dose ml/15 lit of water): Thiomithoxam 25% WG @7gm, Imidacloprid 17.8 % SL @12ml,

Profenophos 50 EC @30ml

7. Spiraling whitefly (*Aleurodicus dispersus*)

Life cycle: Egg-Nymph-Adult

Control measure(Dose ml/15 lit of water): Removal of host plants, Installation of yellow sticky traps, Release of predators viz., Coccinellid predator, Cryptolaemus montrouzieri, Release of parasitoids viz., Encarsia haitierrsis and E.guadeloupae, Thiomithoxam 25% WG @7gm, Imidacloprid 17.8 % SL @12ml, Dimethoate 30% EC @ 15ml

Banana

1. Rhizome weevil (*Cosmopolites sordidus*)

Life cycle: Egg-Grub-Pupa-Adult

Control measure(Dose ml/15 lit of water): Acephate 75 SP @ 15 gm, Thiamethoxam 12.6% + Lambdacyhalothrin 9.5% ZC @ 10ml, Removal of pseudo stems below ground level

2. Pseudostem borer(*Odoiporus longicollis*)

Life cycle: Egg-Grub-Pupa-Adult

Control measure(Dose ml/15 lit of water): Collect and destroy the damaged and dead plants, Flubendamide 20 WG @ 7.5gm, Emamectin Benzoate 5% SG @ 10ml, Carbofuran 3 G @30 kg/ ha

3. Banana Aphid (*Pentalonia nigronervosa f. typica*)

Life cycle: Egg-Nymph-Adult

Control measure(Dose ml/15 lit of water): Thiomithoxam 25% WG @7gm, Imidacloprid 17.8 % SL @12ml

4. Lace Wing Bug (*Stephanitis typicus*)

Life cycle: Egg-Nymph-Adult

Control measure(Dose ml/15 lit of water): Thiomithoxam 25% WG @7gm, Carbofuran 3 G @15 kg/ha

5. Hard Scale (*Aspidiotus destructor*)

Life cycle: Egg-Nymph-Adult

Control measure(Dose ml/15 lit of water): Pruning of infested branches and burning, Thiamethoxam 12.6% + Lambdacyhalothrin 9.5% ZC @ 10ml

6. Fruit Rust Thrips (*Chaetanaphothrips signipennis*)

Life cycle: Egg-Larva-Adult

Control measure(Dose ml/15 lit of water): Spinosad 45% SC @5-7ml, Spinetoram 11.7% SC @ 15-20 ml

Castor Hairy Caterpiller

7. Pericallia ricini

Life cycle: Egg-Larva-Adult

Control measure(Dose ml/15 lit of water): Profenophos 50 EC @30ml, Thiomithoxam 25% WG @7gm, Use burning torch to kill the congregating larvae

8. Cutworm (*Spodoptera litura*)

Life cycle: Egg-Larva-Pupa-Adult

Control measure(Dose ml/15 lit of water): Flubendamide 20 WG @ 7.5gm,Emamectin Benzoate 5% SG @ 10ml, Novaluton 10 % EC @10ml

Papaya

1. Whitefly (*Bemisia tabaci*)

Life cycle: Egg-Nymph-Adult

Control measure(Dose ml/15 lit of water): Thiomithoxam 25% WG @7gm, Imidacloprid 17.8 % SL @12ml. Dimethoate 30% EC @ 15ml

2. Fruitfly (*Bactrocera dorsalis*)

Life cycle: Egg-Nymph-Adult

Control measure(Dose ml/15 lit of water): Dimethoate 30% EC @ 15ml, Flubendamide 20 WG @ 7.5gm

3. Ash Weevil (*Myllocerus spp*)

Life cycle: Egg-Grub-Adult

Control measure(Dose ml/15 lit of water): Thiomithoxam 25% WG @7gm, Imidacloprid 17.8 % SL @12ml, Carbofuran 3 G @15 kg/ha

4. Green Peach Aphid (*Myzus persicae*)

Control measure(Dose ml/15 lit of water): Thiomithoxam 25% WG @7gm, Imidacloprid 17.8 % SL @12ml, Quinalphos 25 % EC @ 10 ml

Citrus

1. Aphid (*Toxoptera citricida*)

Life cycle: Egg- Nymph- Adult

Control measure(Dose ml/15 lit of water): Thiomithoxam 25% WG @7gm, Imidacloprid 17.8 % SL @12ml, Quinalphos 25 % EC @ 10 ml

2. Citrus Black Fly (*Aleurocanthus woglumi*)

Life cycle: Egg-nymph-Adult

Control measure(Dose ml/15 lit of water): Cloropyriphos 20 EC @1 lit/acre

3. Psyllid (*Diaphorina citri*)

Life cycle: Egg-Nymph-Adult

Control measure(Dose ml/15 lit of water): Cloropyriphos 20 EC @1 lit/acre, It is transmits the "Greening" virus

4. Mealy Bug (*Planoccus citri*)

Life cycle: Egg-Nymph-Adult

Control measure(Dose ml/15 lit of water): Thiomithoxam 25% WG @7gm, Imidacloprid 17.8 % SL @12ml, Profenophos 50 EC @30ml, Use sticky trap (5cm length) on fruit bearing shoots

5. Fruit Sucking Moth (*Otheris maternal*)

Life cycle: Egg-Larva-Pupa-Adult

Control measure(Dose ml/15 lit of water): Dimethoate 30% EC @ 15ml, Flubendamide 20 WG @ 7.5gm, *Bacillus thuringiensis var kurstaki* 2g/lit, Neem oil 10,000 ppm @ 15ml, Trap crop – growing tomato crop in orchards to attract the adult moth, Poison bait: dilute suspension of fermented molasses and malathion 0.05% (50 EC at 1ml/lit)

6. Thrips (*Thrips nilgiriensis*)

Life cycle: Egg-Nymph- Adult

Control measure(Dose ml/15 lit of water): Spinosad 45% SC @5-7ml, Spinetoram 11.7% SC @ 15-20 ml

7. Cottony Cushion Scale (*Icerya purchase*)

Life cycle: Egg-Nymph-Adult

Control measure(Dose ml/15 lit of water): Pruning of infested branches and burning, Thiamethoxam 12.6% + Lambdacyhalothrin 9.5% ZC @ 10ml

8. Leaf Miner (*Phyllocnistic citrella*)

Life cycle: Egg-Larva-Adult

Control measure(Dose ml/15 lit of water): Deltamethrin 2.8% EC @ 15ml, Neem oil 10,000 ppm @ 15ml

9. Butterfly (*Papilio demolious*)

Life cycle: Egg-Larva-Pupa-Adult

Control measure(Dose ml/15 lit of water): First instar - Spraying of 1ml DDVP (Nuvan), Field release of parasitoids *Trichogramme evanescens* and *Telenomus sp* on eggs of *Brachymeria sp* larvae and *Pterolus sp* pupae

Grapes

1. Stem Girdle (*Sthenias grisator*)

Life cycle: Grub-Adult

Control measure(Dose ml/15 lit of water): Thiomithoxam 25% WG @7gm, Imidacloprid 17.8 % SL @12ml, Quinalphos 25 % EC @ 10 ml

2. Flea Beetle (*Scelodonta strigicollis*)

Life cycle: Egg-Grub-Adult

Control measure(Dose ml/15 lit of water): Remove the loose bark at the time of pruning to prevent egg laying, Shake vines to dislodge adult beetles, Carbofuran 3 G at 30 kg/ ha, Thiomithoxam 25% WG @7gm

3. Thrips

Life cycle: Egg-Nymph-Adult

Control measure(Dose ml/15 lit of water): Spinosad 45% SC @5-7ml, Spinetoram 11.7% SC @ 15-20 ml

4. Mealy Bug (*Ferrisia virgata)*

Life cycle: Egg-Nymph-Adult

Control measure(Dose ml/15 lit of water): Thiomithoxam 25% WG @7gm, Imidacloprid 17.8 % SL @12ml, Profenophos 50 EC @30ml, Use sticky trap (5cm length) on fruit bearing shoots

5. Berry Plume Moth (*Oxyptilus regulus*)

Life cycle: Egg-Larva-Adult

Control measure(Dose ml/15 lit of water): Summer ploughing – kill the pupae, Neem oil 10,000 ppm @ 15ml, Deltamethrin 2.8 EC @ 20 ml

Pomegranate

1. Anar Butterfly (*Deudorix isocrates*)

Life cycle: Egg-Larva-Adult

Control measure(Dose ml/15 lit of water): Female – V shaped patch on forewing, Collect and destroy caterpillars in the early stage of attack, Conserve parasitoids like *Cotesia glomeratus*, Quinalphos 25 % EC @ 10 ml

2. Fruit Borer (*Conogethes punctiferalis)*

Life cycle: Egg- Larva- Pupa- Adult

Control measure(Dose ml/15 lit of water): Novaluton 10 % EC @10ml, Neem oil 10,000 ppm @ 15ml, Flubendamide 20 WG @ 7.5gm, Emamectin Benzoate 5% SG @ 10ml, *Bacillus thuringiensis* 30 gm, HNPV 1.5 x 10^{12} POBs/ ha, Trap Crop : Merigold

3. Tailed Mealy Bug (*Ferrisia virgate)*

Life cycle: Egg-Nymph-Adult

Control measure(Dose ml/15 lit of water): Thiomithoxam 25% WG @7gm, Imidacloprid 17.8 % SL @12ml, Profenophos 50 EC @30ml

4. Whitefly (*Siphoninus phillyreae*)

Life cycle: Egg-Nymph-Adult

Control measure(Dose ml/15 lit of water): Thiomithoxam 25% WG @7gm, Imidacloprid 17.8 % SL @12ml, Dimethoate 30% EC @ 15ml

5. Aphid (*Aphis punicae*)

Life cycle: Egg- Nymph- Adult

Control measure(Dose ml/15 lit of water): Thiomithoxam 25% WG @7gm, Imidacloprid 17.8 % SL @12ml, Quinalphos 25 % EC @ 10 ml, Yellow Sticky Trap

Pineapple

1. Mealy Bug (*Pseudococcus brevipes*)

Life cycle: Egg-Nymph-Adult

Control measure(Dose ml/15 lit of water): Thiomithoxam 25% WG @7gm, Imidacloprid 17.8 % SL @12ml, Profenophos 50 EC @30ml, Use sticky trap (5cm length) on fruit bearing shoots

2. Rhinoceros beetle (*Oryctes rhinoceros*)

Life cycle: Egg-Grub-Adult

Control measure(Dose ml/15 lit of water): Carbofuran 3 G at 30 kg/ ha, Thiomithoxam 25% WG @7gm, Imidacloprid 17.8 % SL @12ml

Clusterd Apple

1. Fruit Borer (*Deudorix isocrates*)

Life cycle: Egg-Larva-Pupa-Adult

Control measure(Dose ml/15 lit of water): Novaluton 10 % EC @10ml, Neem oil 10,000 ppm @ 15ml, Flubendamide 20 WG @ 7.5gm, Emamectin Benzoate 5% SG @ 10ml, *Bacillus thuringiensis* 30 gm, HNPV 1.5 x 10^{12} POBs/ ha, Trap Crop : Merigold

2. Citrus Fruitfly (*Papilio demolious*)

Life cycle: Egg-Nymph-Adult

Control measure(Dose ml/15 lit of water): Dimethoate 30% EC @ 15ml, Flubendamide 20 WG @ 7.5gm

Aonla

1. Leaf Roller (*Caloptilia acidula*)

Life cycle: Egg-Larva-Adult

Control measure(Dose ml/15 lit of water): Dimethoate 30% EC @ 15ml, Quinalphos 25 % EC @ 10 ml

2. Fruit borer (*Deudorix isocrates*)

Life cycle: Egg-Larva-Pupa-Adult

Control measure(Dose ml/15 lit of water): Novaluton 10 % EC @10ml, Neem oil 10,000 ppm @ 15ml, Flubendamide 20 WG @ 7.5gm, Emamectin Benzoate 5% SG @ 10ml

3. Fruit Piercing Moth (*Othreis maternal*)

Life cycle: Egg-Larva-Pupa-Adult

Control measure(Dose ml/15 lit of water): Use light trap, Destruction in kerosenised water below such light, Use of poison baits or carbaryl 2g/l

4. Bark Borer (*Indarbela tetraonis*)

Life cycle: Egg-Larva-Adult

Control measure(Dose ml/15 lit of water): Apply Copper Oxychloride paste on trunk, Carbofuran 3 G @30 kg/ ha

5. Aphid (*Setaphis bougainvilleae*)

Life cycle: Egg- Nymph- Adult

Control measure(Dose ml/15 lit of water): Thiomithoxam 25% WG @7gm, Imidacloprid 17.8 % SL @12ml

Quinalphos 25 % EC @ 10 ml, Yellow Sticky Trap

6. Whitefly (*Trialeurodes rara*)

Life cycle: Egg-Nymph-Adult

Control measure(Dose ml/15 lit of water): Thiomithoxam 25% WG @7gm, Imidacloprid 17.8 % SL @12ml, Dimethoate 30% EC @ 15ml

7. Mealy Bug (*Ferrisia virgata*)

Life cycle: Egg-Nymph-Adult

Control measure(Dose ml/15 lit of water): Thiomithoxam 25% WG @7gm, Imidacloprid 17.8 % SL @12ml, Profenophos 50 EC @30ml

Apple

1. Wooly Aphid (*Eriosoma lanigerum*)

Life cycle: Egg- Nymph- Adult

Control measure(Dose ml/15 lit of water): Thiomithoxam 25% WG @7gm, Imidacloprid 17.8 % SL @12ml, Quinalphos 25 % EC @ 10 ml, Yellow Sticky Trap

2. San Jose Scale (*Quadraspidiotus perniciosus*)

Life cycle: Egg-Nymph-Adult

Control measure(Dose ml/15 lit of water): Encourage the activity of parasitoids *Prospaltella perniciosi*, Select nursery stock free scale infestation

3. Codling Moth (*Cydia pomonella*)

Life cycle: Egg-Larva-Adult

Control measure(Dose ml/15 lit of water): Banding - corrugated cardboard bands should be applied to tree trunks, Acetamiprid 20% SP @ 5 gm, Use sex pheromone trap, Release egg parasitoids, Trichogramma embryophagum at 2000/tree

4. Cottony Cushion Scale (*Icerya purchasi*)

Life cycle: Egg-Nymph-Adult

Control measure(Dose ml/15 lit of water): Pruning of infested branches and burning, Thiamethoxam 12.6% + Lambdacyhalothrin 9.5% ZC @ 10ml

5. Stem Borer (*Apriona cinera*)

Life cycle: Egg-Grub-Adult

Control measure(Dose ml/15 lit of water): Novaluton 10 % EC @10ml, Neem oil 10,000 ppm @ 15ml, Flubendamide 20 WG @ 7.5gm, Emamectin Benzoate 5% SG @ 10ml

Plum

1. Peach Borer (*Sphenoptera lafertei*)

Life cycle: Egg-Grub-Adult

Control measure(Dose ml/15 lit of water): Novaluton 10 % EC @10ml, Neem oil 10,000 ppm @ 15ml, Flubendamide 20 WG @ 7.5gm, Emamectin Benzoate 5% SG @ 10ml, Swab trunk with carbaryl 50 WP at 0.2%

2. Plum Beetle (*Anomala lineatipennis*)

Life cycle: Egg-Grub-Adult

Control measure(Dose ml/15 lit of water): Carbofuran 3 G at 30 kg/ ha, Thiomithoxam 25% WG @7gm, Imidacloprid 17.8 % SL @12ml

3. San Jose Scale (*Quadraspidiotus perniciosus*)

Life cycle: Egg-Nymph-Adult

Control measure(Dose ml/15 lit of water): Encourage the activity of parasitoids: *Prospaltella perniciosi*

Select nursery stock free scale infestation

Pear

1. Stem Borer (*Sahydrassus malabaricus*)

Life cycle: Egg-Larva-Adult

Control measure(Dose ml/15 lit of water): Collect and destroy the damaged and dead plants, Flubendamide 20 WG @ 7.5gm, Emamectin Benzoate 5% SG @ 10ml

2. Aphid (*Dilachnus krishn*)

Life cycle: Egg- Nymph- Adult

Control measure(Dose ml/15 lit of water): Thiomithoxam 25% WG @7gm, Imidacloprid 17.8 % SL @12ml, Quinalphos 25 % EC @ 10 ml

Peach

1. San Jose Scale (*Qudraspidiotus perniciosus)*

Life cycle: Egg-Nymph-Adult

Control measure(Dose ml/15 lit of water): Encourage the activity of parasitoids: *Prospaltella perniciosi,* Select nursery stock free scale infestation

2. Green Peach Aphid (*Myzus persicae)*

Life cycle: Nymph- Adult

Control measure(Dose ml/15 lit of water): Thiomithoxam 25% WG @7gm, Imidacloprid 17.8 % SL @12ml, Quinalphos 25 % EC @ 10 ml

3. Peach Borer (*Sphenoptera lafertei)*

Life cycle: Egg-Grub-Adult

Control measure(Dose ml/15 lit of water): Novaluton 10 % EC @10ml, Neem oil 10,000 ppm @ 15ml, Flubendamide 20 WG @ 7.5gm, Emamectin Benzoate 5% SG @ 10ml, Swab trunk with carbaryl 50 WP at 0.2%

ꙮ

Fruit Crop Disease

Mango

1. Anthracnose (*Colletotrichum gloeosporioides)*

Fungal

Control measure(Dose ml/15 lit of water): Copper oxychloride 45 gm, Carbendazim 50 % 35 gm

2. *Powdery Mildew* (Oidium mangiferae/ Acrosporum mangiferae)

Fungal

Control measure(Dose ml/15 lit of water): Hexaconazole 5% SC 30 ml, Hexa 4% + Zineb 35 gm, Wettable sulphur @ 0.2%

3. Mango Malformation (*Fusarium moliliforme* var. *subglutinans)*

Fungal

Control measure(Dose ml/15 lit of water): Reduced by spraying 100-200ppm NAA during October, Carbendazim 50 % 35 gm

4. Stem End Rot (Diplodia natalensis)

Fungal

Control measure(Dose ml/15 lit of water): Copper oxychloride 45 gm + Streptomycin 2 gm, Bordeaux Mixture 2 %

5. Red Rust (*Cephaleuros virescens)*

Fungal

Control measure(Dose ml/15 lit of water): Hexaconazole 5% SC 30 ml, Tebuconazole 25.9 WW, Pyroclostrabin 5%+ Matiram 55% WG

6. Grey Blight (Pestalotia mangiferae)

Bacterial

Control measure(Dose ml/15 lit of water): Copper oxychloride 45 gm + Streptomycin 2 gm, Bordeaux Mixture 2 %

7. Sooty mould (*Capnodium mangiferae)*

Fungal

Control measure(Dose ml/15 lit of water): The fungus grows on the leaf surface on the sugary substances secreted by jassids, aphids and scale insects, Copper oxychloride 45 gm + Streptomycin 2 gm, Thiomithoxam 25% WG @7gm, Imidacloprid 17.8 % SL @12ml

Banana

1. Anthracnose (*Gloeosporium musarum*)

Fungal

Control measure(Dose ml/15 lit of water): Copper oxychloride 45 gm, Carbendazim 50 % 35 gm, Banana bunches should be harvested at correct stage of maturity

2. Banana Bract Virus

Transmitted by AControl measure(Dose ml/15 lit of water): phid

Control measure(Dose ml/15 lit of water): Thiomithoxam 25% WG @7gm, Imidacloprid 17.8 % SL @12ml

3. Banana Bunchy top Virus

Transmitted by Aphid

Control measure(Dose ml/15 lit of water): Thiomithoxam 25% WG @7gm, Imidacloprid 17.8 % SL @12ml

4. Sigatoka (*Mycospharella musicola)*

Fungal

Control measure(Dose ml/15 lit of water): Carbendazim 50 % 35 gm, Hexaconazole 5% SC 30 ml, Hexa 4% + Zineb 35 gm

5. Wrinia rot (Erwinia carotovora *sub sp.* carovora)

Bacterial

Control measure(Dose ml/15 lit of water): Copper oxychloride 45 gm + Streptomycin 2 gm, Bordeaux Mixture 2 %

6. Panama Wilt (*Fusarium oxysporum f.sp cubense)*

Fungal

Control measure(Dose ml/15 lit of water): *Pseudomonas fluorescens @ 2.5kg/ha,* Copper oxychloride 45 gm + Streptomycin 2 gm

ꕤ

Guava

1. Anthracnose (*Colletotrichum gloeosporioide)*

Fungal

Control measure(Dose ml/15 lit of water): Copper oxychloride 45 gm, Carbendazim 50 % 35 gm

2. Rust (*Puccinia psidii* Symptom)

Fungal

Control measure(Dose ml/15 lit of water): Hexaconazole 5% SC 30 ml, Tebuconazole 25.9 WW, Pyroclostrabin 5%+ Matiram 55% WG

3. Algal Leaf Spot (*Cephaleuros virescens)*

Fungal

Control measure(Dose ml/15 lit of water): Carbendazim 50 % 35 gm, Hexaconazole 5% SC 30 ml, Hexa 4% + Zineb 35 gm

ꕤ

Sapota

1. Leaf Spot (*Phaeoleospora indica)*

Fungal

Control measure(Dose ml/15 lit of water): Copper oxychloride 45 gm, Carbendazim 50 % 35 gm

2. Sooty Mould *(Capnodium sp.)*

Fungal

Control measure(Dose ml/15 lit of water): The fungus grows on the leaf surface on the sugary substances secreted by jassids, aphids and scale insects, Copper oxychloride 45 gm + Streptomycin 2 gm, Thiomithoxam 25% WG @7gm, Imidacloprid 17.8 % SL @12ml

ꕤ

Grapes

1. Downy Mildew (*Plasmopara viticola)*

Fungal

Control measure(Dose ml/15 lit of water): Mencozeb 45 gm, Hexaconazole 5% SC 30 ml, Tebuconazole 18.3% SC @ 25ml, Metalaxyl + Mancozeb 0.4 %

2. Powdery Mildew (*Uncinula necator)*

Fungal

Control measure(Dose ml/15 lit of water): Hexaconazole 5% SC 30 ml, Hexa 4% + Zineb 35 gm, Wettable sulphur @ 0.2%

3. Bird's eye Spot/Anthracnose *(Gloeosporium ampelophagum Elsinoe amphelina)*

Fungal

Control measure(Dose ml/15 lit of water): Copper oxychloride 45 gm, Carbendazim 50 % 35 gm

IV

Soil

TYPES OF SOIL

- There are seven soil deposits in India
- Alluvial Soil
- Black Soil
- Red and Yellow Soil
- Laterite Soil
- Arid Soil
- Forest Soil

i. Alluvial Soil:

- The rivers deposit very fine particles of soil in different parts of India. This type of soil is widespread in Northen Plain of India.
- Alluvial soils are rich in humus as they are deposited by three important river of Himalaya, Indus river, Ganges river. They are found in the eastern coastal plains of India, particularly in the deltas of rivers Mahanadi, Godavari river and Kaveri.
- These are generally rich in Phosporic acis, lime and potash, and is well known for its water holding capacity which makes it ideal for growing sugarcane, paddy, wheat and other cereal crops.

v. Black Soil:

- This type of soil is black in colour. These soils are also called as regur soils.
- The soil is suitable for growing cottons, due to which it is also known as black cotton soil.
- It is believed that the climatic conditions along with the parent rock material are the important factors for the formation of black soil.
- They cover the plateaus of Maharashtra, Saurashtra, Malwa, Madhya Pradesh, Chhattisgarh and extend in South-East direction along Godavari and Krishna valleys.
- These soils contain essential clay minerals as montmorillonite.
- They are made up of clayey materials. They are well known for their capacity to hold moisture. They are rich in calcium carbonate, magnesium, potash and lime. During summer, they develop crack. This is very helpful for aeration of black soil.

v. Red Soil:

- Red soil is a type of soil that develops in a warm, temperate, moist climate under deciduous or mixed forest, having thin organic and organic-mineral layers overlying a yellowish-brown leached layer resting on an alluvium red layer.
- Red soils are generally derived from crystalline rock.
- They are usually poor growing soils, low in nutrients and humus and difficult to cultivate because of its low water holding capacity.
- It is one of the most fertile soil which grows all type of plants

v. Laterite Soil:

- Laterite soils are formed from chemical decomposition of rocks.
- Soil mainly contain iron oxide which gives them characteristic pink or redcolor.
- These soils are found in Central, Eastern and Southern India. These are residual soils is formed from basalt and have high specific gravity.
- These soils are mostly composed as calcite depositions. They are more suitable for crops like cashew nut

v. Arid Soil:

- Arid soils range from red to brown in color.
- They are generally sandy in texture and saline in nature. In some areas the salt content is very high and common salt is obtained by evaporating the water.
- Due to the dry climate, high temperature, evaporation is faster and the soil lacks humus and moisture.
- The lower horizons of the soil are occupied by Kankar because of the increasing calcium content downwards.
- The Kankar layer formations in the bottom horizons restrict the infiltration of water. After proper irrigation these soils become cultivable as has been in the case of western Rajasthan.

v. Forest Soil:

- Forests soils are found in the hilly and mountainous areas where sufficient rainforests are available.
- The soils texture varies according to the mountain environment where they are formed.
- They are loamy and silty in valley sides and coarse grained in the upper slopes.
- In the snow covered areas of Himalayas, these soils experience denudation and are acidic with low humus content.
- The soils found in the lower parts of the valleys particularly on the river terraces and alluvial fans are fertile

SOIL SAMPLING

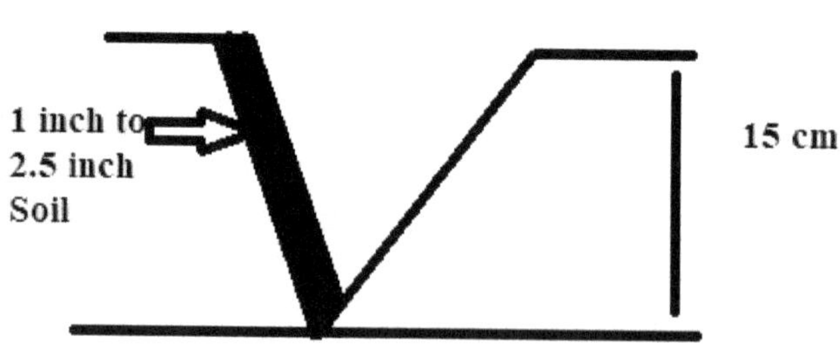

- Soil samples should be taken in zig-zag pattern
- Avoid to take samples from dead furrow, wet spot area near main bud trees, manufacture heaps and irrigation channels
- For shallow rooted crops take up to 15 cm depth and in case of deep rooted crops up to 30 cm depth
- Do "V" shape cut of 15 cm depth and take sample

SOIL TEXTURE AND SOIL STRUCTURE

Parameter	Saline	Alkaline	Saline-Alkaline
EC (ds/m)	>4	<4	>4
ESP (%)	<15	>15	>15
pH	7-8.5	>8.5	8.5
Deficiency	Ca, K	Fe, Mn, P, Zn	
Toxicity	Na, Cl	Na, B	
Control	Gypsum	Gypsum, Calcium Chloride	

- Soil Texture: It include three size of soil particle like Sand, Silt and Clay
- Soil Structure: It include structure like Blocky, Granular, Platy, Crumb, Massive etc.
- Soil structure can be changed soil texture can't change
- To maintain soil pH in case of alkaline soil(>7 pH) add gypsum @8 Qt/ha and Iron pyride (FeS_2) @12 Qt/ha.
- To maintain acidic soil add lime in the soil

V

Nursery

NURSERY

- Nursery is the place where plants are cared during the early stage of growth and providing optimum condition for better germination and subsequent growth until they are strong to be planted out in their permanent place.

- Types of Nursery:

1. Based on time period

- Temporary Nursery: Seasonal
- Permanent Nursery: Commercial

1. Based on plant growth:

- Fruit Plant Nursery
- Vegetable plant nursery
- Ornamental plant nursery
- Medicinal and Aromatic plant nursery
- Forest plant nursery
- Hi-tech nursery
- Agriculture crop nursery

3. Based on structure of nursery

- Open nursery
- Closed nursery

4. Based on landscape

- Horizontal nursery
- Vertical nursery

5. Based on type of sale

- Retail nursery
- Wholesale nursery
- Private nursery

GROWING MEDIA

- Growing media is other than soil material in which plants are grown.
- Use/Benefit of growing media:

1. Optimum rooting environment for physical stability
2. Storage of air for root
3. Water availability when plants needed
4. Nutrient supply for root and plant growth

- Due to relatively shallow depth and limited volume of container, media must be amended to provide appropriate physical and chemical properties to plant

- Growing media:

1. Peat and peat like material
2. Wood residues
3. Bagasse
4. Rice Husk
5. Organic material
6. Coir pith

7. Sand
8. Clay
9. Perlite
10. Vermiculite
11. Calcium clays
12. Expanded polystyrene
13. Urea formaldehydes

1. Peat and peat like material:

- Peat moss is formed by accumulation of plant material in paddy drained areas
- Sphagnum moss: dehydration remains of acid bog plants from the genus. It is light in weight and has ability to absorb 10-20 times of its weight in water
- It contains specific fungicide substance which accounts for its ability to inhibit damping off of seedling. Drainage and aeration are improved in heavier soil while moisture and nutrient retention are increase in lighter soil
- Black peat: plant is submerged in water, lower side of black layer peat is called lack peat which is used in all horticulture crops and we should remove upper side of peat monthly or weakly which is called white peat

2. Wood Residues:

- It is a byproduct of lumber industry
- Nitrogen depletion is problem during soil decomposition
- Leaf mold and saw dust also used
- Bark: Properly similar to sphagnum moss which is used in orchid cultivation

3. Bagasse:

- Byproduct of sugar industry
- Increase aeration and drainage

4. Rice Husk:

- Byproduct of rice milling industry
- Nitrogen depletion is not serious problem
- Good drainage capacity

5. Organic material:

- Organic material used as media are corn cobs, straws, peanut, pecan shells, etc.
- It increases aeration and nutrient level
- Provide organic nutrient for batter plant growth

6. Coir pith:

- Obtained by mechanical processing of coconut husk
- Good water storage capacity
- It is used as sowing, propagation and potting media

7. Sand:

- 0.05 mm to 2 mm diameter
- Improve flow ability and add weight where needed
- Make easy water movement

8. Clay:

- Clay act as nutrient buffer
- With clay it's possible to add nutrient without reaching to high salinity level

9. Perlite:

- Siliceous material of volcanic origin
- To prepare perlite first used crushed grade, then heat until light powdery substance occur
- Lightness and uniformity make perlite very useful for increasing aeration, drainage and water uptake
- Perlite is dry and float on top of container during irrigation

10. Vermiculite:

- Micaceous material produced by heating
- Vermiculite particle is like plate
- Very high water holding capacity and aeration and having good drainage capacity
- Excellent exchange and buffering capacity as well as ability to supply potassium and magnesium

11. Calcium clay:

- Heating of montmorillonite clay
- High calcium exchange and water holding capacity

12. Expanded Polystyrene:

- Byproduct of polystyrene
- Increase aeration and decrease bulk density

13. Urea formaldehydes:

- Heavy water holding capacity

VI

Plant Propogation

SEXUAL PROPAGATION

- Propagation of plant is the involvement of science and art in a skillful way. Basic knowledge and skill of it can be a better source of income through commercial nurseries
- Plants can be propagated by sexual and asexual means. Sexual means includes propagation by seeds, while asexual propagation is based on the utilization of vegetative parts of plants for raising new ones.
- Propagation or multiplication of plants by seeds is known as 'sexual propagation'

- Advantages:

    - It is an easy, simple and convenient method of plant propagation
    - Plants propagated by seeds live longer, are vigorous and more resistant to biotic and abiotic stresses
    - It is the only means of creating genetic diversity of plants
    - Seeds can be transported easily and stored for a longer time using this method
    - Some plants like papaya, marigold, chili, capsicum, tomato, etc., cannot be propagated by asexual method

- Disadvantages:

- Plants that are propagated through seeds have long gestation period, which results in delayed flowering and fruiting
- Sexually propagated plants show variations and are not genetically true-to-type to the mother plants
- Plants grow vigorously and cause obstruction in intercultural practices like harvesting and spraying
- Crop species, which do not produce seeds like pineapple, banana, fig, jasmine, bougainvillea, etc., cannot multiply by this method

ASEXUAL PROPAGATION

- It is also called "vegetative propagation"
- The vegetative parts of a plant like leaf, stem, root or their modified forms are used for propagation. Most of the horticultural crops are commercially propagated by vegetative or asexual method of propagation

- Advantages:

  - Plants propagated by sexual propagation re rue-to-type genetically
  - Maturity is uniform and the plant gives quality yield
  - Plants propagated by sexual method are small in size, so praying of chemicals and harvesting are easy
  - This method enables noble plant production, e.g., different colors of flowers in single rose plant and different types of mangoes in one mango plant can be produced through sexual method only

- Disadvantages:

  - By vegetative propagation, new varieties cannot be developed
  - It requires specialized skills, so it is an expensive method of propagation
  - The life span of asexually propagated plants is short as compared to sexually propagated ones
  - These plants are more prone to biotic and abiotic stresses

- Asexual propagation can be done with different method like:
    - Cutting
    - Layering
    - Grafting
    - Budding

ꕤ

CUTTING

- Cutting is a detached vegetative part of a plant, which on separation and planting is able to regenerate the missing parts and develop itself into a new plant. It is an inexpensive and quick method of propagation
- The method is named after the part of plant used for cutting, e.g., stem, root and leaf
- Stem cutting Based on the age and maturity of shoots detached for vegetative propagation, stem cuttings is of four types:

1. Hardwood cutting
2. Semi-hardwood cutting
3. Softwood cutting
4. Herbaceous cutting

1. Hardwood cutting:

- Such a cutting is taken from woody plants
- Mostly, deciduous plants are propagated by this method
- One-year old mature branch is cut into pieces of suitable sizes and planted in the rooting medium, e.g., rose, grapes, fig, pomegranate, bougainvillea, lagerstroemia, jasmine, hibiscus, etc.

2. Semi-hardwood cutting:

- A semi-hardwood cutting is taken from 4 to 9-month old shoots of current season woody plants
- Most ornamental foliage plants like croton, acalyphas, aralias, diffenbachia, russelia, cestrum, nerium, etc., are propagated by semi-

hardwood cuttings.

3. Softwood cutting:

- Such a cutting is taken from herbaceous or succulent plants
- Shoots of 2 to 3-month old plants are selected for softwood cuttings examples are alternanthera, coleus, duranta, clerodendrum, etc.

4. Herbaceous cutting:

- Such a cutting is taken from herbaceous plants.
- Shoots of 1 to 2-month old plants are selected for herbaceous cuttings examples are chrysanthemum, iresine, pilea, dahlia, petunia, carnation, marigold, etc.

- **Leaf cutting** selection of cutting Plants with thick fleshy leaves having buds are propagated by leaf cutting
  - Vegetative buds are present in the notches of leaf margin (bryophyllum) or on the vein (begonia rex)
  - Leaf blade or pieces of it with bud are put on the rooting medium under favourable conditions
  - In case of black raspberry, the leaf blade, along with petiole and a short piece of the stem with attached axillary buds, are kept in the medium for rooting
  - Plants like snake plant (senseveria), blackberry, rhododendron and bryophyllum are propagated by this method.

LAYERING

- It is an attached method of propagation
- In this method, roots are allowed to develop on the covered portion of the stem while still being attached to the mother plant
- After the emergence and development of the roots, this portion is separated from the mother plant and allowed to grow as a new plant on its own root stem. Such root stem is known as 'layer'.

- Types of layering
  - Simple layering
  - Compound or serpentine layering
  - Trench layering
  - Mound layering or stooling
  - Air layering
- Simple layering:
  - In simple layering, a partial tongue-like cut is given on a branch
  - The branch is then bent to the ground and the treated portion is covered with soil, keeping the top or terminal portion exposed
  - The layered branches produce roots in weeks and are ready for transplanting in a nursery after detaching them carefully. Examples are jasmine, ixora, clerodendron, pyrostegia, etc.
- Compound or serpentine layering:
  - Compound layering is similar to simple layering, except the branches are alternately covered and exposed along their length
  - The branches must be longer so that they can be layered at several places
  - This method is followed in plants like bougainvillea, jasmine, clematis, muscadine grape and wisteria
- Trench layering:
  - Trench layering is primarily used in fruit plants
  - Covering the shoots with soil results in etiolation, so it is also known as 'etiolation layering'. New shoots arise from the length of the burried branches
  - After rooting, individual shoots are separated from the mother plant. This method is followed in apple, cherry, pear, jasmine and rhododendron.
- Mound layering or stooling:

- This method is followed in plants whose branches are firm and difficult to bend
- The selected plant must be at dormant stage at the time of layering

- Air layering:

  - It is also known as 'gootee'. Examples are Ficus elastica, Callistemon, croton, monstera, citrus fruits, lychee, philodendron, pomegranate, etc.

GRAFTING

- The method of joining parts of two plants in a manner that they form a unit and function as one plant is known as grafting
- Advantages:

  - Plants propagated by grafting are true-to-type, and bear flowers and fruits early
  - The plants can be multiplied and preserved by grafting
  - Local variety of older plants can be improved to superior variety by top working
  - Wounded or damaged tree trunks can be repaired by special grafting methods
  - Rootstock has an influence on resistance, vigour and quality of grafted plants

- Disadvantages:

  - It requires specialized skill
  - It is an expensive method of propagation
  - New varieties cannot be developed by grafting
  - Plants produced through grafting are short lived as compared to plants propagated by seeds
  - When contaminated tools or propagation material are used in grafting, newly propagated plants may also get infected

- **Rootstock**
  - The part of the graft that provides root system to the grafted plant is known as rootstock
  - It is, normally, raised by seeds in the seedbed, and then, transplanted in the nursery bed for budding and grafting
  - Rootstocks are also raised in pots and polythene bags
- Characteristics of rootstock
  - Adaptable to local climatic conditions
  - Resistant to adverse climatic and soil conditions
  - Resistant or tolerant to pests and diseases
  - Propagates easily
  - Compatible with scion
  - Promotes early healing and formation of cambium layer
- **Scion**
  - The upper portion of graft combination taken from the desired plant to be multiplied is known as scion
- Characteristics of scion
- Scion wood must be of the previous season but not from more than one-year old plant
- Flowering shoots or shoots from where the harvesting is recently done must be avoided
- Healthy and well-developed vegetative buds must be selected
- The scion or bud sticks must be selected from known performing orchard trees
- Types of grafting:

  i. Scion attached method
    - Approach grafting
    - Tongue grafting

v. Scion detached method

   - Veneer grafting
   - Side grafting
   - Wedge or cleft grafting
   - Stone or epicotyl grafting
   - Whip or splice grafting
   - Bark grafting

1. **Scion attached method:**

- In this method, the scion shoot is not detached from the mother plant until the union takes place
- After the successful union of the scion and rootstock, the scion is separated in gradual cut from the mother plant
- For making the grafting handy, the rootstock is grown in a container or polythene bag
- This method is followed in plants, in which successful graft unions are difficult to obtain

- Approach Grafting:

- Approach grafting is also known as "inarching"
- The main feature of approach grafting is that two independent self-sustaining plants are grafted together
- After the successful union of the graft, the scion plant is detached below the graft union from the mother plant and the top of the rootstock plant is removed above the graft
- This method is useful for plants, in which successful graft unions are difficult to obtain
- This method is, usually, performed for plants growing in a container, as well as, big trees. In the latter case, the rootstock seedling is brought near the scion branch by erecting a platform

- Tongue Grafting:

   - Bring the selected rootstock and scion close together
   - Find out the most comfortable point of contact

- Remove a slice of wood along with a 2.5 to 5-cm long bark from the rootstock and scion
- A second slanting partial cut downward on the stock and upward on the scion is made, producing a thin tongue-like structure of the same size on the stem of the stock and the scion
- Insert the scion in the stock so that these tongue cuts interlock
- All operated portions must be in contact with each other
- Tie the operated portions

2. Scion detached method:

- This method is a more popular method of grafting and comparatively easier to perform
- Besides, the rate of success of plant propagation is more in this case. In this method, the scion is first detached from the mother plant, and then, inserted or tied on the rootstock

Veneer Grafting

- It is a simple and economical method of grafting
- It the most ideal method for establishing in situ orchards and top working of old unproductive orchards
- The best time in north India for veneer grafting is March–April and July–August
- Veneer grafting differs from side grafting
- In this, the vertical flap of the stock is completely removed and a slanting cut is given on one side of the scion
- Mango, cashew and peach are commercially propagated by this technique

Side Grafting

- In this method, the operated scion is inserted into the side of the established rootstock, which has more girth than the scion, e.g., hibiscus

Cleft Grafting

- It is comparatively a simple and an easy method of grafting, which is widely used in fruit trees, e.g., mango, jackfruit, bael, amla, etc.

Stone or epicotyl Grafting

- This method is commonly adopted for the rapid multiplication of mango plants
- In this method, stones (seeds) are sown in polythene bags or moist sand bed and covered with 5 to 7-cm layer of leaf mould for germination
- When the seedlings are about 15 days old, they are taken out and grafted indoor

Whip or splice Grafting

- It is the oldest method of grafting. This method is used in fruit trees like apple, pear, walnut, etc.

Bark Grafting

- A plant graft made by slitting the bark of the stock and inserting the scion beneath it is called 'bark grafting'. It is commonly used in top working

Bridge grafting

This method is used for repairing wounds in trees made by implements, frost, rodents or diseases

- In this grafting, the bark of a tree is damaged, resulting into girdling
- A completely girdled tree will die
- Bridge grafting repairs girdling

BUDDING

- Budding is the process of inserting a single mature scion bud into the stem (rootstock) in a way that results into a union and continues to grow as a new plant. It is also a type of grafting

- Types of budding:

  - T-budding
  - Patch budding
  - Ring budding
  - Flute budding
  - Forkert budding
  - Chip budding

T – Budding

- T-shaped incision is made for bud insertion on the rootstock, it is called T – budding
- T – budding is also called "shield budding" as the bud used for insertion is in the shape of a 'shield'. It is widely used for propagating fruit trees and ornamental plants. In this method, the rootstocks of compatible plants are raised in beds or poly bags
- Examples are rose, apple, pear, peach, apricot, cherry, sweet orange, etc.

Patch Budding

- A rectangular patch of bark is completely removed from the internodes of the stock plant
- A similar patch of bark with a healthy bud is removed from the scion bud stick
- This patch is placed on the cut portion of the stock and wrapped with a polyethylene strip, keeping the bud exposed
- Examples are amla, mango, jamun, rubber, etc.

Ring Budding

- In this method, a bark of approximately 3–6 cm wide in ring form is removed from the stock
- The same dimension of bark with a healthy bud is removed from the scion bud stick and placed on the stalk
- After placing the ring in position, tie it with a polythene strip, keeping the bud exposed, e.g., ber and cherry.

Flute Budding

- This is a slight modification of ring budding. Instead of removing the complete ring, a narrow portion of the bark about 1/8 of its circumference is left on the stock
- A similar portion of the scion is removed along with the bud and is fitted on the cut portion of the stock
- The bark of the stock and bud are tied with a polyethylene strip, exposing the growing point e.g., ber

Forkert Budding

- Examples are cashew nut, jackfruit, mango, etc.

Chip Budding

- This is mostly practised in February–March
- Fruits like apple, grapes and pear can be propagated through this technique

TISSUE CULTURE

- It is a technique for growing plant tissues isolated from the parent plant in an artificial medium and controlled environment over a prolonged period under aseptic conditions.
- It is used on commercial scale in gerbera, orchid, banana, carnation, anthurium, etc. It is based on the phenomenon of 'totipotency' of a cell, which denotes the capacity of a plant cell to regenerate into a full-fledged plant having different organs.
- Examples are banana, papaya, gerbera, carnation, rose, orchid, etc

SPECIALIZED ORGANS

Specialized Organ	Modification of	Examples
Bulb	Stem	onion, tuberose, amaryllis
Corm	Stem	gladiolus, crocus
Tuber	Stem or Root	root tuber like dahlia, caladium, dioscorea, Jerusalem artichoke, etc.; and stem tuber like begonia, potato, etc.
Rhizome	Stem	canna, ferns, ginger
Sucker	Shoot	chrysanthemum (stem), Clerodendron splendens (root suckers), anthurium, etc.
Tuberous Root	Root	satavar, dahlia, chlorophytum, etc.
Runner	Stalk	doob grass, strawberry, chlorophytum, etc.

TRAINING AND PRUNING

- Training:
- Training is a practice in which tree growth is directed into a desired shape and form.
- Training young fruit trees is essential for proper tree development. It is better to direct tree growth with training than to correct it with pruning
- The goal of tree training is to direct tree growth and minimize cutting
- Mainly concerned with giving a form or shape to the plant
- Determines the general character and even details of the plant's outline and of its branching and framework
- Training includes summer training and summer pruning as well as dormant pruning
- The goal of tree training is to direct tree growth and minimize cutting

- **Objectives:**

    - To admit more sunlight and air to the center of the tree and to expose maximum leaf surface to the sunlight.
    - To direct the growth of the tree so that various cultural operations, such as spraying and harvesting are performed at the lowest cost.
    - To protect the tree from sunburn and wind damage.

- To secure a balanced distribution of fruit bearing parts on the main limbs of the plant

- **Pruning:**
- Pruning is the proper and judicious removal of plant parts such as shoots, spurs, leaves, roots or nipping away of terminal parts etc. to correct or maintain tree structure and increase its usefulness
- It is done to
  - Make the plant more productive and bear quality fruits,
  - Increase longevity of the tree,
  - Make it into manageable shape and
  - To get maximum returns from the orchard
- Pruning is a dwarfing process and can be used to maintain any desired tree size
- Removal of a branch removes not only stored carbohydrates but reduces the potential leaf surface as well
- Pruning increases fruit size, nitrogen per growing point and stimulates growth near the cut.
- Excessive pruning reduces fruitfulness especially with young vigorous trees that may already be developing too much vegetative growth.
- Large cuts results in excessive stimulation of sprouts near the cut, while well distributed small cuts spreads the stimulus better over the entire tree.
- The severity, kind and amount of pruning to be done on a tree depend on the
  - age,
  - existing framework,
  - condition of bark and wood,
  - Growth characteristics
  - Fruiting habit of the variety
  - Whether tree is permanent or filler
- Pruning is most often done during the winter, commonly referred to as dormant pruning

- Objective:

  - To control the size of the plant.
  - To control the form (structural makeup of the plant) which involves number, placement, relative size and angle of branches.
  - Better quality fruits by better light distribution.
  - To remove diseased, dried and broken branches.
  - To remove the non-productive parts in order to divert the energy into those parts that are capable of bearing fruits.
  - Proper proportion of root- shoot ratio.
  - To regulate the fruit crop.
  - Longevity of the tree.
  - Chances of insects-pests, diseases and winter injury are less

VII

Hormones & PGR

Hormones

Plant hormones are organic substances that regulate plant growth and development. These are the components which are available in very low quantity in plants but the role of hormones is very specific and irreplaceable.

- Major types of plant hormone:

1. Auxin
2. Gibberellin
3. Cytokinins
4. Ethylene
5. Abscisic Acid (ABA)

1. Auxin:

- Works on plant growth specially leaves and stem
- Basically do cell enlargement or elongation
- Generally found in meristem and shoot tip
- Auxin moves top to bottom so help in increase vegetative growth
- Stem bending occur due to higher concentration of auxin at darken side of stem
- High level of auxin above lateral bud block their growth. If the shoot tip is removed lateral buds begin to grow
- Auxin helpful for formation of gibberellic acid and cytokinin

- PGR that Auxin inhibitor:
  - Synthetic: IBA, NAA, 2-4-D
  - Natural: IAA

1. Gibberellin:

- Produced in shoot apex and primarily in leaf bud
- Works on cell division and cell elongation
- Involved in overcoming dormancy in seed and buds
- Gibberellic acid easily moves in both directions in plants because it not only produced in shoot apex but also in root structure
- It helpful in seed germination and increase fruit set also
- Promote male flower in cucumber
- Overcoming cold requirement for some seed give treatment of gibberellic acid forgoes the cold requirement
- Gibberellic acid in cauliflower increase curd size

3. Cytokinen:

- Promote cell division and found in all tissues for cell division (embryo, seed, fruit, etc.)
- Upward movement of Cytokinen occur in plant (Root to shoot)
- Interact with auxin to influence differentiation of tissue also used to stimulate bud formation
- Role in new bud activation and expansion
- In tissue culture Cytokinen used for shoot development
- Prevent leaf senescence (leaf ageing and leaf fall)
- Prevent yellowing by stabilizing the content of protein and chlorophyll in leaf

4. Ethylene:

- Produce in actively growing meristem of plant
- Works in senescing, ripening or ageing fruis-flowers and seed germination
- In certain plant tissue as a response to bending, wounding and bruising
- Promote leaf senescing and leaf fall

- Increase female flower in cucumber
- Responsible for degreening of citrus fruit and breakdown the chlorophyll content

5. Abscisic Acid (ABA):

- Widespread in plant body
- Moves readily through plant so it's called plant stress hormone
- ABA synthesized by leaves
- Promoting effect of auxin and gibberellin
- Involved with leaf and fruit abscission
- ABA is effective in including closure of stomata in leaves, including role in stress physiology in plants
- Inhibit mRNA and synthesis of protein

PGR- Plant Growth Regulators

Plant growth regulators (PGRs) are chemicals used to modify plant growth such as increasing branching, suppressing shoot growth, increasing return bloom, removing excess fruit, or altering fruit maturity. Numerous factors affect PGR performance including how well the chemical is absorbed by the plant, tree vigour and age, dose, timing, cultivar, and weather conditions before, during, and after application.

- PGR and classes
- Auxin: IAA, NAA, IBA, 2-4-D, 4-CPA
- Gibberellins: GA_3 (Gibberellic Acid)
- Cytokinin: Kinetin, Zeatin
- Ethylene: Ethereal
- Abscisic Acid: Dormins, Phaseic Acid

- **HORMONES – PGR AND USES**

Sr. No	Physiological Action	Growth Controller
1	Seed germination	GA_3, Kinetin
2	Tuber storage, Increase tuber self-life	Melic hydrazine, ABA, 2-4-5 T
3	Increase bud dormancy period	ABA, CCC
4	Physiological Action	Growth Controller
5	Stop sucker growth in Banana, Guava	2-4-D, NAA
6	Early flowering	GA_3, NAA, 2-4-D, CCC
7	Sex transformation	GA_3, PBA, Ethephone
8	Fruit growth	NAA, 2-4-D, GA_3, Kinetine
9	Adventitious root growth	NAA, IBA, 2-4-D, IAA
10	Early fruit ripening	Ethephone, Ethylene
11	Increase fruit self-life	GA_3, Kinetine
12	Increase self-life of leafy vegetables	GA_3, Kinetine
13	Reduce fruit, leaves, flower dropping	NAA, GA_3, 2-4-D
14	Leaves, fruit, flower senescing	ABA, Ethephone, Ethylene, NAA, GA_3
15	Control vegetative growth	GCC, Cultar
16	Weed control	Paraquot, Propanol, MCPA, 2-4-D, Diuron

VIII

Post Harvest Technology

Importance

- Agricultural processing may be defined as an activity, which is performed to maintain or improve the quality or to change the form or characteristics of the agricultural product. Processing operations are undertaken to add value to agricultural materials after their production. The main purpose of agricultural processing is to minimize the qualitative and quantitative deterioration of the material after harvest
- Post harvest loss reduction technology encompasses the usage of optimum harvest factors, reduction of losses in handling, packaging, transportation and storage with modern infrastructure machinery, processing into a wide variety of products, home scale preservation with low cost technology
- Adoption of these techniques could make available a large quantity of food by avoiding losses and provide better quality food and nutrition, more raw materials for processing, thus ensuring better returns to the farmers
- Importance of Post-harvest technology lies in the fact that it has the capability to meet food requirement of growing population by eliminating losses making more nutritive food items from raw commodities by proper processing and fortification
- Post-harvest technology has potential to create rural industries. India, where 80 percent people live in the villages and 70 percent of them depend on agriculture has experienced that the process of industrialization has shifted the food, feed and fiber industries to urban

areas

- Value addition to food products has assumed vital importance in our country due to diversity in socio-economic conditions, industrial growth, urbanization and globalization
- **Primary processing:** Purification of raw materials by removing foreign matter, immature grain and then making the raw material eligible for processing by grading in different lots or conversion of raw material into the form suitable for secondary processing.
- **Secondary processing:** Processing of primary processed raw material into product which is suitable for food uses or consumption after cooking, roasting, frying etc.
- **Tertiary processing:** Conversion of secondary processed material into ready to eat form

PRODUCT TRACEBILITY

- Traceability is the procedure of tracking (and documenting) all your raw materials, parts, and finished goods throughout your manufacturing process "when and where the product was produced by whom."
- Traceability has been defined in the ISO 9001 standard from the International Organization for Standardization
- Importance:
- If a product quality problem occurs, the manufacturer of the product must take effective measures promptly
- A slow or ineffective response from the manufacturer will create a sense of distrust among consumers or business partners, which may even endanger the existence of the company
- In addition, as laws to protect consumers have been implemented, the number of companies required to quickly recall their products due to problems has been increasing every year
- Benefits:
  - Increase quality
  - Improve product recalls
  - Improve inventory tracking

- Improve food safety
- Improve customer service
- Respond to consumer demand
- Verify harvest date and location

CARYOPRESERVATION

- Storage of living organism at ultra-low temperature such that it can be revived and restored to the same living state as before it was stored
- Liquid nitrogen at -195°C has been standard for long term preservation

CALCIUM NITRATE BANNED

- Calcium carbide is banned now a day but the reason is $CaCO_3$ can also affect the neurological system by including prolonged hypoxia
- The FSSAI has banned $CaCO_3$ under prevention of Food Adulteration Act, 1954

IX

Farming

ZERO BUDGET NATURAL FARMING

- Addressing the United Nations Conference on desertification (COP-14), Indian PM told the global community that India is focusing on ZBNF. It was also highlighted in budget 2019 in the bid to double farmer's income by 2022.
- Zero Budget Natural Farming is method of chemical free agriculture.
- It was promoted by agronomist Subhas Palekar
- It aims to bring down the cost of production to nearly zero and retune to a pre-green revolution style of farming
- ZBNF claims that no need for expensive input such as fertilizer, pesticide and intensive irrigation

- ZBNF is based on 4 pillars:

    - Jeevamrutha
    - Bijamrita
    - Acchadana (Mulching)
    - Whapasa: It is a condition where, there are both air molecules and water molecules present in the soil. There by helping in reducing water requirement.

- Humus: To increase soil fertility. 1 kg humus absorb 6 liter of water from air and supply to root.

- Benefit of ZBNF:

  - The cost of production could be reduced and farming made into a zero budget exercise. (According to National Sample Survey office (NSSO) data almost 70% of agricultural households spend more than they earn.
  - Chemical & intensive farming is resulting in soil & environmental degradation, a ZBNF environmental friendly so definitely a timely initiative.
  - Promotes soil aeration, mineral watering, inter cropping, mulching etc. discourage intensive irrigation and deep ploughing
  - ZBNF suits in all crops and all climatic zone.

- In July, 2018 AP rolled out an ambitious plan to became India's first state to practice 100% Natural farming by 2024.

- Issues of ZBNF:

  - Sikkim (India's 1st organic state) seen some decline in yield
  - Many farmers return to conventional farming seeing their ZBNF returns drop after few years
  - Improve soil fertility but in case of productivity still some problem in ZBNF
  - CBNF advocates the need of an Indian breed cow, whose number are declining at a fast pace.

- Government Initiatives:

  - RS. 500 Cr announced under the Paramparagat Krishi Vikas Yojana in the year of 2020-21.
  - Rs. 12.5 Cr announced under Natural Project on Organic Farming in the year of 2020-21.
  - Rs. 175 Cr announced under Organic value chain for North Eastern Region on the year of 2020-21.
  - Organic farming marketed by Jaivik kheti Portal

PRECISION FARMING

- Precision farming is a farming management concept based on observing, measuring and responding to inter and intra-field variability in crops. The goal of precision agriculture research is to define a decision support system for whole farm management with the goal of optimizing returns on inputs while preserving resources.

- **Advantages:**

  - GPS allows fields to be surveyed with ease.
  - Yield and soil characteristics can be mapped.
  - Non-uniform fields can be sub-divided into smaller plots according to their specific requirements.
  - Provides opportunities for better resource management and so could reduce wastage.
  - Minimizes the risk to the environment particularly with respect to nitrate launching and groundwater contamination via the optimsation of agrochemical products.

- **Disadvantages:**

- Techniques are still under development and so it is important to take specialist advice before making expensive decisions.
- Initial capital costs may be high and so it should be seen as a long-term investment.
- It may take several years before you have sufficient data to fully implement the system.
- Extremely demanding work particularly collecting and then analyzing the data.

ORGANIC FARMING

- Organic farming which is a holistic production management system that promotes and enhances agro-ecosystem health, including biodiversity, biological cycles, and soil biological activity is hence important.

- Organic farming is a production system which avoids the use of synthetically compounded fertilizers, pesticides, growth regulators, genetically modified organisms and livestock food additives.
- To the maximum extent possible organic farming system rely upon crop rotations, use of crop residues, animal manures, legumes, green manures, off farm organic wastes, biofertilizers, mechanical cultivation, mineral bearing rocks and aspects of biological control to maintain soil productivity to supply plant nutrients and to control insect, weeds and other pests.
- Significant difference in soil health indicators such as nitrogen mineralization potential and microbial abundance and diversity, which were higher in the organic farms also.
- The increased soil health in organic farms also resulted in considerably lower insect and disease incidence.
- In organic farming, it is important to constantly work to build a healthy soil that is rich in organic matter and has all the nutrients that the plants need. Several methods viz. green manuring, addition of manures and bio fertilizers etc. can be used to build up soil fertility.
- These organic sources not only add different nutrients to the soil but also help to prevent weeds and increase soil organic matter to feed soil microorganisms.
- Organic manure is used as fertilizer in organic farming like FYM and vermicompost etc. which are generally low in nutrient content, so high application rates are needed to meet crop nutrient requirements.
- Green manuring with Sesbania, cowpea, green gram etc are quiet effective to improve the organic matter content of soil.
- There are some substances can supply essential nutrients and may be from plant, animal, microbial or mineral origin and may undergo physical, enzymatic or microbial processes and their use does not result in unacceptable effects on produce and the environment including soil organisms.
- There are some biological control also available in organic farming which are Rhizobium, Azotobactor, Azospirillum, Micorhizal fungi, blue green algae, etc.

- Advantages of Organic Farming:

    - To keep agricultural production at a sustainable level

- to maintain environment health by reducing the level of pollution.
- Resists soil erosion, holds water better and thus requires less irrigation.
- To improves the soil physical properties such as granulation, good tilth, good aeration, easy root penetration and improves water-holding capacity and reduces erosion.
- To improves the soil's chemical properties such as supply and retention of soil nutrients, reduces nutrient loss into water bodies and environment and promotes favorable chemical reactions.

- Limitations of Organic Farming:

    - Organic manure is not abundantly available and on plant nutrient basis it may be more expensive than chemical fertilizers if organic inputs are purchased.
    - Production in organic farming declines especially during first few years, so the farmer should be given premium prices for organic produce.
    - We require bulky material in case of organic farming
    - Marketing of organic produce is also not properly streamlined

SUSTAINABLE AGRICULTURE

- Sustainable Agriculture means simply which...

    - Satisfy human food and fiber needs
    - Enhance environmental quality and the natural resource base upon which the agriculture economy depends
    - Make the most efficient use of nonrenewable resources and on-farm resources and integrate, where appropriate, natural biological cycles and controls
    - Use of resources on basis of current requirement and future need to maintain the agriculture.

- Advantages:

    - Cost reduction
    - Control of pollution
    - Save biodiversity
    - Soil erosion
    - Saving of natural resources

- Disadvantages:

    - More skilled person required
    - Bigger consumption of time and effort
    - Lower income at initial stage

X

General Agriculture

ISSUES IN AGRICULTURE SECTOR

- Agriculture sector dealing with so many issues, some of them are mentioned below which effect directly or indirectly to the farmers or farming.
- Low productivity
- Declining average size of farm holding
- More dependency on rainfall
- Lack of easy credit to the farmers
- Fragmented Supply chain:
    - Large gap in storage and supply chain
    - Limited connectivity of required resources
    - Lack of marketing infrastructure
- Neglect of crop rotation
- Inadequate use of manure and fertilizer
- Loss of land in Agriculture due to it's convert in non-agriculture is became major issue now a day
- Fragmentation of land is problem- small farmers share their produce at farm gate not in APMC
- 55% Agro workers are work for wages
- 45% farmers are cultivating their own land
- Water guzzling crops:
- 1 kg Sugar require 1500-2000 lit water and1 kg Rice require 5000 lit water

- As per Indian data producer estimate positive in graph (Producer estimate means production per acre of land which is comparatively good)
- While consumer estimate is negative (Consumer estimate means price per unit of produce is low) Which means farmers are producing good but comparatively there are not getting good price. In India consumer rate is 0.87% while in China it is 1.10% due to PDS system. (Data extracted from OECD)
- MSP is majorly fevers wheat and rice crop so farmers getting more benefits also so need to modify cropping pattern also.
- Milk producer and farmers growing fruits and vegetables are equally prone to fluctuation in Market price.

- Solution:

  - Development initiative including infrastructure, technological and intervention farm mechanization.
  - Improve allied sectors like Horticulture, Food processing, Poultry, etc.
  - Co-operative farming

GLOBLE IMPACT OF CLIMATE CHANGE ON HORTICULTURE CROPS

- Climate change and agriculture related to each other, specific temperature range and climate change is required for growth of specific crop
- Climate change means affect in temperature, extreme climate condition like heat waves, drought, low or excessive rainfall, ozone concentration at ground level and change in sea level.
- Studies suggest that even small change in climate will cause 30% decline in agriculture productivity
- Global warming also affects productivity

  - The temperature is rise in Indo genetic plain has affected wheat crops. State like Jarkhand, Odisha, Chatisgadh, registered 40% less production in rice
  - Increase aridity: 15% of semi-arid regions would actually experience conditions similar to arid climates today

- CO_2 study: Increasing CO_2 level does increase crop yield, if nothing else is considered, especially for C_3 plants both through CO_2 fertilization and reduce respiration as the pores close at higher temperature but it also changes climate, drought and aridity which decrease crop yield
- CO_2 level also effect on C_3 and C_4 plants.

- Assume new areas are opened up to Agriculture,

  - Climate specialist found that while at present on 32% of the boreal region is stable for agriculture which is by 2099 roughly 76% in the world

- C_3, C_4 and CAM photosynthesis:

  - C_4 method is more able to use CO_2 then C_3, and more efficient to all temperature and CAM system mainly for many fruit crops except pineapple
  - So, C_4 method is better at converting CO_2 in to plant mass for same level of sunlight
  - CAM system works better in dry condition

- Climate change impact on Horticulture crops:

  - A study conducted at IISR, Calicut using GIS models have shown that many areas presently suitable for spices would become unsuitable in another 25 years
  - There would be new areas which are presenting unsuitable, become highly suitable for cultivation of spices
  - The requirement of annual irrigation will increase and heat unit required will be achieved in much lesser time
  - Pollination will be affected adversely because of higher temperature. Floral abortions flower and fruit drop will be accrued frequently
  - Higher temperature will reduce tuber initiation process in Potato, reduced quality in tomatoes and pollination in many crops. In case of crucifers it may lead to bolting, anthocyanin production may be affected in apple and capsicum. Tip burn and blossom end rot will be the common phenomenon in tomatoes.

REVOLUTIONS IN AGRICULTURE

Yellow Revolution	Oil seed Production (Especially Mustard and Sunflower)
Protein Revolution	Higher Production (Technology driven 2nd Green Revolution)
Black Revolution	Petroleum Products
Blue Revolution	Fish Production
Brown Revolution	Leather/ Cocoa
Golden Fiber Revolution	Jute Production
Golden Revolution	Fruits/ Honey Production/ Horticulture Development
Grey Production	Fertilizers
Pink Revolution	Onion Production
Evergreen Revolution	Overall Production
Silver Revolution	Egg / Poultry Production
Silver Fiber Revolution	Cotton
Red Revolution	Tomato Production
Round Revolution	Potato
Green Revolution	Food Grains
White Revolution / Operation Flood	Milk Production
Sweet Revolution	Honey Production

ꕤ

ATMANIRBHAR BHARAT ABHIYAAN

- Government launches 20 Lakh package for Rural economy development
- The concept of ABA was integrated with the announcement of the economic package to tackle the corona virus pandemic. Under the mission, special provision have been made for the poor, including migrants and farmers. Some of these are.
- 25 lakh new Kisan Credit Card sanctioned with a loan limit of Rs.25000 crore
- Support provided under Rural Infrastructure Development Fund to states
- Rs. 3 Lakh crore emergency credit for MSMEs
- Various benefits have been also given under MUDRA scheme
- The wage rate under MGNREGA has been increased to Rs. 202
- Free food grain supply is also being provided to the migrants

- Through Pradhan Mantri Kisan Yojana, Rs. 2000 has been transferred directly to the 8.7 crore farmers
- The main focus of the government is "Vocal for Local". Locally available products will be given importance in order to promote the rural economy
- The Government schemes in sync with the Aatmanirbhar Bharat Abhiyaan:
    - Coir Udyami Yojana
    - Skill Upgradation and Mahila Coir Yojana
    - Prime Minister's Employment Generation Programme
    - PM Awas Yojana
    - Deen Dayal Antyodaya Yojana
    - UJALA 2019
    - PM Kaushal Vikas Yojana
    - Ayushman Bharat
    - PM Matsya Sampada Yojana
- Primary transportation would include movement from farm to Mandis, FPO Collection Centre and Warehouse etc.
- Secondary transportation would include movement from Mandis to Intra state & Interstate mandis, Processing units, Railway station, warehouses and wholesalers etc.
- This app also facilities traders in transportation of perishable commodities by Reefer vehicles
- Under the extra ordinary situation prevailing in the country currently due to lockdown, "Kisan Rath" will ensure smooth and seamless supply linkages
- To help improve value realization especially in triable areas "Kisan Udaan" will be launched by the Ministry of Civil Aviation
- In May, 2020 the finance minister had announced Rs. 30,000 crore additional emergency working capital for farmers through NABARD and Rs. Two lakh crore credit boost to 2.5 crore farmers under Kisan Credit Card Scheme.

DOUBLING THE FARMERS' INCOME

- There are some basic support provided to farmers from Indian Government to prove the objective of doubling the farmers' income.
- Supporting contract farming by promulgation of Model Contract Farming Act, Up-gradation of Garmin Haats to work as centers of aggregation and for direct purchase of agriculture commodities
- Providing e-NAM to farmers
- Progressive market reforms
- Distributing soil health cards
- PM Krishi Sinchayee Yojana (PMKSY) "Per drop more crop"
- Better insurance coverage under Pradhan Mantri Fasal Bima Yojana (PMFBY)
- Making loans available to farmers at a reduced rate of 4 % annum and extending the facility of Kisan Credit Card for animal husbandry and fisheries related activities to the farmers
- Increase in the Minimum Support Price (MSP)
- Providing the old age Pension of Rs. 3000 to the eligible small and marginal farmers

GI TAG

GI is name or sign used on certain products which corresponds to a specific geographical location or origin

Produce having GI Tag

- WB: Darjeeling Tea
- Bihar: Shahi Litchi
- Bihar: Katarrni Rice
- Bihar: Jardalu Mango
- Bihar: Magahi Paan
- Kerala: Navara Rice
- HP: Kangra Tea
- KT: Nanjangud Banana
- UP: Allahabad Surkha-Guava
- TN: Tall Coconut Ethomozy
- WB: Laxman Bhog Mango
- WB: Himsagar Mango
- KT: Robusta coffee

- UP: Dassehri Mango
- India: Basmati Rice
- Gujarat: Gir Kesar Mango
- KT: Banglour Blue Grapes
- KT: Onion
- Gujarat: Bhaliya Wheat
- Darjeeling Tea was first indian product to get GI Tag (2004-05)

- Latest GI Tag- Kashmir- Saffron & Manipuri black rice
- GI are covered as a component of intellectual property rights (IPRs) under the Paris Convention for the protection of Industrial Property
- At National Level, GI is governed by the world trade organization (WTO) agreement on trade- Related Aspects of Intellectual Property Rights (TRIPS)
- In Indian GI registration is don administered by GI of goods (Registration & Protection) Act, 1999 which come into force with effect from September, 2003
- Head Quarter: Chennai

- Benefits:
    - Legal Protection of products
    - Prevent unauthorized use of GI Tag products by others
    - Promotes the economic prosperity of producers of GI Tag goods by enhancing their demand in national and international market
    - Social & economic benefit (For food products- supply chain and value chain development- so that Tourism can also boost)
    - Boost the export

- How GIs are protected:
    - Special law for the protection of GTs or appellation of origin
    - Trademark laws in form of collective marks
    - Consumer protection laws
    - Laws against unfair competition

- Organizations:

- To promote the protection of intellectual property in world

- WIPO: World Intellectual Property Organizations
- Member: 185
- HQ: Geneva, Switzerland

- Registration Process:

    - Step 1.Filling of Application
    - Step 2. Primary security and examination (One month)
    - Step 3. Show cause Notice (Two month)
    - Step 4. Publication in the geographical Indication Journal (Within 3 month)
    - Step 5. Opposition to registration (Not necessary)
    - Step 6. Registration (Accepted GI)
    - Step 7. Renewal (GI valid for 10 years)

- Renew by payment of renewal fee.

SHOULD AGRICULTURE SUBSIDIES TO BE STOPPED OR NOT

- According to mu opinion agriculture subsidy should not be stopped as our agriculture contribute 15% to our GDP and 60% to total employment beside it we know that our economy is agriculture dependent
- 85% farmers come under small and marginal land holding farmers who are not able to do without subsidies
- We know that Agriculture input is crucial thing for cultivation of land and our farmers can't afford that much of costly input
- I think instant of stopping agriculture subsidy we should focus on implementation of subsidy and farmers reach out of subsidy
- Along with these farmers can afford the costly fertilizer which is important factor to increase yield also and if government will not provide subsidy then how farmers can produce and fulfill the consumption need of India.

- Obstacles for the farmers:

- Indian farmers have less land and are basically illiterate or less educated
- Obstacles to understand and apply the technology
- Government subsidy don't reach to themselves as a large part of the subsidies are that by the middlemen or bought by the rich farmers
- Gambling is done during monsoon
- The infrastructure of storing crop like cold storage is not available on every area, this is why 30% of yearly production of vegetables in India are rotten

- Government should take appropriate steps to face these challenges:
    - Higher rate of subsidies to the marginal and lower to rich farmers
    - Provide appropriate teaching of innovative methods to every farmers
    - Growth of canal and tank irrigation
    - The government should also inspect the proper distribution of subsidy

- This is how government should meet the challenges and ensure the farm productivity.

BIOLOGICAL CONTROL OF PEST

i. Biological control of sucking pest:

- Use of natural enemy
- Use of predators:
    - Crysoperla carnia : feed larva and used in control of aphid and jassid
    - Lady bird beetle: 50000 count/acre for the control of aphid
    - Encarsia: Used to control of whitefly
    - Beuvria basiana: 60 g/pump or 1 kg/acre
    - Verticilium leccani
    - Metarhiziyam Anisopli: 60 g/pump

- Neem oil: 5000 ppm, 10000 ppm, use 12-15 ml/pump
- Use of sticky traps: 6-8 traps/acre

v. Biological control of larva:

- Use of pheromone traps
- Fruit fly trap for fruit: 40/ha or 6-8/acre
- Clue lure for cucurbits
- Use of neem oil
- Use of HNPV (Helocoverpa Nuclear Polyhydrosis Virus) and SNPV (Spodoptera Nuclear Polyhydrosis Virus)
- Use of BT Power- 60-70 g/pump
- Use of Beuvria basiana:
- Use of parasitoids:
    - Tricocard: Made with tricoderma: Apply on lower side of leaf and adult will became after 7 days from card

BIOLOGICAL CONTROL OF DISEASE

- Biological control of fungal disease
- Soil application of tricoderma
- Spray of Basilas saptilis and neem oil
- Soil solarization
- Growing of non-host crop
- Use of FYM enrichment with tricoderma
- In case of coconut use FYM enrichment with metarhyziyam due to Rhinoceros beetle

JIVAMRUT

Jivamrut is so nutritive for plants as well as soil so we can use as substitute of fertilizer.

- Procedure:

10 liter of cow urine
+
10 kg of cow dung
+
1 kg Live soil (Bacteria rich soil)
+
1 kg sugar jaggery
+
1 kg gram flour

- Mix all the ingredients properly in 200 liter of water drum and cover it with gunnnybag
- Mix properly twice in a day in clockwise manner
- In case of simmer it takes about 2-3 days to prepared while in case of winter it takes 1 week.
- We can use it for 15 days after prepared.

- How to use:
- Use 200 liter of Jivamrut in one acre of land. We can use in drip also and for spray also.
- Benefits:
- Increase bacteria population in soil which improve soil fertility
- Create micro-climate near plant
- Beneficial earthworm's activity
- Increase Nitrogen level

- Apart from these we can use Nimastra, Brahmastra, Agnistra and Dasparni ark for control of sucking pest.
- Bijamrut, Sunthamrut and strong buttermilk we can use as fungicide.

BORDEAUX MIXTURE

- Bordeaux mixture is used as fungicide and bactericide in plants.
- Uses: Applicable to tomato, potato, chilli, other vegetables, fruits (orange, lime, lemon), beetel vine, ginger, flower and ornamental plant diseases such as foot rot, stem rot, leaf spot, leaf blight, anthracnose, canker,

damping off, black spot, downy mildew, late and early blight etc.

- Procedure for 1% BM preparation:

  1 kg copper sulphate ($CuSO_4$) in 50 liter of water
  +
  1 kg Slaked lime ($Ca(OH)_2$) in 50 liter of water
  +
  Add in 100 liter of water
  (1% stock solution is ready)

- Concentration of $CuSO_4$, $Ca(OH)_2$ and water in different form of Bordeaux Mixture...

  - BM: 1:1:100 (1% stock solution)
  - BP (Bordeaux Pest): 1:1:10 (10% stock solution)
  - For Fruit: 6:6:100 (6% stock solution)
  - For Vegetables: 3:3:100 (3% stock solution)

- The original formula developed by Millardet contains 5 lbs of $CuSO_4$ + 5lbs of lime + 50 gallons of water. The chemistry of Bordeaux mixture is complex and the suggested reaction is: $CuSO_4 + Ca(OH)_2 = Cu(OH)_2 + CaSO_4$

- Advantages:

  - Very easy and can prepared by farmers themselves.
  - Can act as fungicide, bactericide and algaecide.
  - The chemicals required for this is copper sulphate and lime which is easily available in the market.
  - All the diseases controlled by copper based fungicides such as leaf spot, blight diseases can be controlled by this.
  - It is less toxic to human as compare to other commercial fungicides.

- Disadvantages:

  - It cannot be keep for long periods (More than 2 days after preparation).

- It cannot be applied during the cold and cloudy weather, as it causes phytotoxicity to plants.
- It cannot be applied to apple, maize and some of the dwarf rice varieties.

AREA MAPPING

- 1 ha = 6.25 Bigha
- 1 ha= 2.5 Acre
- 1 Acre= 2.5 Bigha
- 1 meter= 3.28 feet
- 1 Bigha= 16 Guntha = 131.2 * 131.2 feet
- No. of Plant/ha= 10,000/m*m
- No. of Plant/acre= 43560/ft*ft

LD_{50} AND KD_{50}

- LD_{50}:
  - LD_{50} stands for Lethal Dose
  - It is the amount of material(Pesticide) given all at once, which cause the death of 50% of a group of test animals.
- KD_{50}:
  - KD_{50} stands for Knock Down
  - It measures quick knock down effect. Which means chemical take how much time to control the insect population.

Product Label	Toxicity Level	Oral LD_{50}	Dermal LD_{50}	Listed Chemicals
Red Label	Extremely	1-50	1-200	Monocrotophos, Zinc Phosphate, Ethyl mercury acetate, etc.
Yellow Label	Highly	51-500	201-2000	Endosulfan, Carbary quinalphos
Blue Label	Moderate	501-5000	2001-20,000	Malathion, Glyphosate
Green Label	Slightly	>5000	>20,000	Mancozeb, Oxyfluorfen, etc.

PREDATOR, PARASITE, PARASITOID

- Predator:
- Size: Generally bigger then host
- Kills more than one host at a time or during lifecycle.
- Ex. Lady bird beetle

- Parasitoid:
- Size: Generally smaller then host
- They complete their one stage of whole life cycle inside the host, and later they kill the host.
- So Kills one host during the whole lifecycle.
- Ex. Tricograma

- Parasite:
- They survive on host for complete their lifecycle
- They may kill or may not kill the host
- Ex. Mosquitoes, Roundworms, some viruses, Ticks, etc.

IPM: Integrated Pest Management

- Integrated pest management, or IPM, is a process you can use to solve pest problems while minimizing risks to people and the environment
- It focuses on long-term prevention of pests or their damage through a combination of techniques such as biological control, habitat manipulation, modification of cultural practices, and use of resistant varieties

- In IPM approaches for grater effectiveness:

  - Biological Control
  - Culture Control
  - Mechanical and Physical Control
  - Chemical Control

- How to do IMP control for any crop:

  - Set Action Thresholds: Before taking any pest control action, IPM first sets an action threshold, a point at which pest populations or environmental conditions indicate that pest control action must be taken. Sighting a single pest does not always mean control is needed. The level at which pests will become an economic threat is critical to guide future pest control decisions.

  - Monitor and Identify Pests: Not all insects, weeds, and other living organisms require control. This monitoring and identification removes the possibility that pesticides will be used when they are not really needed or that the wrong kind of pesticide will be used.

  - Prevention: Prevention in IPM means using cultural methods, such as rotating between different crops, selecting pest-resistant varieties, and planting pest-free rootstock. These control methods can be very effective and cost-efficient and present little to no risk to people or the environment.

  - Control: IPM programs first evaluate the proper control method both for effectiveness and risk. Effective, less risky pest controls are chosen first, including highly targeted chemicals, such as pheromones to disrupt pest mating, or mechanical control, such as trapping or weeding. If further monitoring, identifications and action thresholds indicate that less risky controls are not working, then additional pest control methods would be employed, such as targeted spraying of pesticides.

INM: Integrated Nutrient Management

- Integrated Nutrient Management refers to soil fertility and of plant nutrient supply at an optimum level for sustaining the desired productivity through optimization of the benefits from all possible sources of organic, inorganic and biological components in an integrated manner\

- Importance of Integrated Nutrient Management:

    - Nutrient management helps to reduce contamination to waterways by plant nutrients
    - Improve soil fertility
    - Enhance plant productivity
    - Reduce the cost of chemical fertilizers
    - Providing balanced nutrition to crops
    - Promotes carbon sequestration and prevents the deterioration of soil, water, ecology, and also leaching of nutrients from the soil

Schemes

RKVY-RAFTAAR

- Rastriya Krishi Vikash Yojna- Remunerative Approach for Agriculture and Allied sector Rejuvenation.
- The NDC (National Department Council) confirmed 4% annual growth rate in Agriculture sector and plan for RKVY in 29th May, 2007.
- RKVY turned in to RAFTAAR in the year of 2017.
- This scheme is centrally sponsored scheme. The amount sponsored by central and state is:

  Central : Stare = 60 : 40
  Central : State = 90 : 10 in case of Hilly areas.

- Ministry involved in this scheme is Ministry of Agriculture and farmer welfare.

- Objectives:

1. Risk mitigation and strengthening the efforts of farmers along with promoting agribusiness entrepreneurship through the creation of agri-infrastructure.
2. Providing all the state with autonomy and flexibility in making plans as their local need.
3. Helping farmers in increasing their income by encouraging productivity and promoting value chain addition linked production models.

4. To reduce risk of farmers by focusing on increasing the income generation through mushroom cultivation, integrated farming, floriculture, etc.
5. Empowering the youth through various skill development, innovation and agribusiness model.

- List of allied sector covered under RKVY:

1. Crop Husbandry
2. Animal, Dairy, Fisheries
3. Agriculture research & education
4. Agriculture marketing
5. Food storage & warehousing
6. Soil & water conservation
7. Agriculture Financial Institute
8. Agri programs & cooperation

- Areas of focus under RKVY:

1. Integrated development of food crops, cereals, pulses, and millets
2. Agriculture mechanization
3. Soil health & Productivity
4. IPM
5. Horticulture
6. Animal husbandry, dairy & fisheries
7. Sericulture
8. Study tours of farmers
9. Organic & bio fertilizer
10. Innovative schemes

- RKVY-RAFTAAR is umbrella scheme. Below are some major sub scheme:
- Bringing Green Revolution to Eastern India (BGREI)
- Crop Diversification Program (CDP)
- Reclamation of Problem Soil (RPS)
- Foot & Mouth Disease- Control Program (FMD-CP)
- Saffron Mission
- Accelerated Fodder Development Program (AFDP)

PMFBY: Pradhan Mantri Fasal Bima Yojana

- Pradhan Mantri Fasal Bima Yojana
- Launch date: 13 Jan, 2016
- Launch place: Sherpur, Madhya Pradesh
- Launch by: PM Modi
- Introduced by: Arun Jaitely
- Introduced in: Union Budget 2016-17
- Guideline release: 18th Feb, 2016
- Budget: 2016-17: 1240 cores, later amount raised to Rs. 5500 cr. In 2017-28 it will be 9000 cr. And In 2018-19 1300 cr.

- Challenges:

  - Currently coverage stands at 23% government aims 50%, lack of awareness needs to be cover.
  - Crop insurance scheme sector is marred by frauds need to take care of this.
  - Centre's state financial liability is estimated to go up.
  - Exclusion of farmers need to be tackled
  - Since compensation will be paid directly to farmers account, there is need to estimate financial infrastructure.

- Objective:

  - To provide insurance coverage & financial support to farmers in event of failure of any notified crop
  - To stabilize the income of farmers to ensure their sustenance
  - To encourage farmers to adopt innovation/modern practices
  - To ensure credit flow in agrisector

- Highlights of Scheme:

  - Uniform premium to be paid by farmers, in case of Kharif crops 2% , Rabi crops 1.5% and for Horticulture crops it is 5%.
  - There is no upper limit of premium.

  - For the help of farmers balance premium to be paid by government
  - Use of technology to capture data of crops
  - This scheme also cover exemption from service tax income
  - Post harvest losses also covered
  - The farmers who took loan from government have compulsory join this scheme, but the farmers who haven't take loan can voluntary join the scheme.

- PMFBY comparison with previous scheme:

Feature	NAIS/MNAIS	PMFBY
Premium Rate	High	Low
Crop Insurance covering	Yes	No
Post-Harvest loss	No	Yes
Localized Risk	No	Yes
Technology used in farming	Not Intended	Mandatory
Awareness	No	Yes

(NAIS- National Agriculture Insurance Scheme
MAIS- Modified National Agriculture Insurance Scheme)

৪৩

PKVY: Paramparagat Krishi Vikash Yojna

- Paramparagat Krishi Vikash Yojna or Traditional Farming Improvement Program
- The scheme was initiated in the year of 2015.
- Under PKMY scheme organic farming is supported and promoted through adoption of organic village by cluster approach
- PKVY is an elaborated component of Soil Health Management (SHM) of major project National Mission of Sustainable Agriculture (NMSA)

- Expected Outcome:

  - Promotion of commercial organic farming through certified organic farming

- The produce will be pesticide residue free and will contribute to improve health
- Raise farmer's income and create potential market
- Motivate the farmers for natural resource mobilization for input production

- Program implementation:

  - Firstly, motivate the farmers group to take up organic farming under PKVY.
  - 50 or more than 50 farmers make a cluster under PKVY and make a cluster of 50 acre of land of organic farming. Like this later in 3 years 10000 farmers jointly come together and make 5 lakh acre land of organic farming
  - No liability on farmers for expenditure on certification
  - The government will provide Rs. 20,000/acre in 3 years for seed to harvesting and transport to market to every farmers as financial support
  - Organic Farming will be promoted by using traditional resources and the organic products will also link with market
  - This program will also increase domestic production and certification of organic produce by involving farmers into market chain

PM-AASHA: PradhanMantri Annadata Aay Sanrakshan Abhiyan

- PradhanMantri Annadata Aay Sanrakshan Abhiyan
- Launch date: Sept. 2018
- The three schemes under PMAASHA:

1. The Price Support Scheme (PSS)

- Under PSS, physical procurement of pulses, oilseeds and copera will be done by central nodal agencies
- Besides, NAFED and FCI will also take up procurement of crops under PSS

- The expenditure and losses due to procurement will be done borne by center

1. The Price Deficiency Payment Scheme (PDPS)

- Under PDPS the center process to cover all oilseeds
- The difference between the MSP and actual selling price will be directly paid into the farmers' bank account
- Farmers who sell their crops in recognized mandis within notified period can be benefited from it

3. The Pilot of Private Procurement and stockiest Scheme (PPPS)

- In case of oilseeds states will have the option to roll out PPPS in selected districts
- Under this, a private player can produce crops at MSP when market price drops below MSP
- The private player will then be compensating through a service charge up to maximum of 15% of the MSP
- These three components will complement the existing schemes of the department of food and public distribution
- They relate to paddy, wheat and other cereals and coarse grain where procurement is at MAP now

- **NAFED**

- National Agriculture cooperative marketing Federation of India was established in the year of 1958
- Registered under multistate co-operative societies Act.
- The objective is to promote co-operative marketing of agriculture produce to benefir the farmers

- **FCI**

- The Food Corporation of India was set up under the food corporation Act, 1964 with the following objectives:

- To effective price support operation for safeguarding the interests of the farmers
- To distribution of food grains throughout the country for public distribution system
- To maintaining satisfactory level of operational and buffer stock of food grains to ensure National Food Security

MIDH: Mission for Integrated Development Horticulture

- Mission for Integrated Development Horticulture
- Centrally sponsored scheme: Government of India contribute 85% except Northen India states and state contribution is 15%, while in case of northen state Government of India contribute 100%

- Objectives:

  - To promote holistic growth of horticulture sector, include all sector of horticulture
  - To encourage aggregation of farmers into farmer's groups like FPOs, FPCs to bring economy of scale and scope
  - To enhance horticulture production, farmers' income and strengthen nutrient security
  - To improve productivity by way of quality germplasm, planting material and water use efficiency through micro irrigation
  - Support skill development and create employment generation opportunities for rural youth in horticulture and post-harvest management specially in cold chain sector

- Sub Scheme:

  - National Horticulture Mission (NHM)
  - Horticulture Mission for North East and Himalayan States (HMNEH)
  - National Bamboo Mission (NBM)
  - National Horticulture Board (NHB)
  - Coconut Development Board (CDB)
  - Central Institute for Horticulture (CIH)

- Activities for which financial assistance is provided
- Setting up for nurseries, tissue culture lab/unites, seed production
- Area expansion of garden-orchard
- Protected cultivation
- Organic farming and certification
- Creation of water resources structure and watershed management
- Bee-keeping for pollination
- Horticulture mechanization
- Creation of Post-Harvest Management marketing infrastructure

NHB: National Horticulture Board

- It was set up in 1984 on the basis of recommendation of the " Group on Perishable Agriculture Commodities" headed by Dr. M.S. Swaminathan
- HQ: Gurugram
- Objective: To improve integrated development of horticulture industry and to help in coordination sustaining the production and processing of fruits and vegetables

KISAN SURYODAY YOJNA

- The scheme was initiated on 75th anniversary of United Nation on 24th Oct, 2020
- Starting from Dahod, Junagadh and Gir somnath district of Gujarat
- The government will provide electricity from morning 5AM to night 9 PM
- Electricity will be provided in two slot of 8 hrs
- Installing transmission infrastructure by 2023
- There will be 17.25 lakh farmers will be beneficiary of this scheme

PMKSY: Pradhamnantri Krishi Sinchayee Yojna

- Pradhamnantri Krishi Sinchayee Yojna
- The scheme was initiated at 1st July, 2015
- Objectives:
  - "Har khet ko pani"
  - More crop per drop
  - Water conservation
  - End to end solution
- PMKSY prepared DIP and SIP (DIP- District Irrigation Plan and SIP- District Irrigation Plan)
- Amount weightage between center and state is 75:25 and in case of Northen east region and hill state 90:10
- Fund allotted for this scheme is:
  - 2015-16: Rs. 5300 Cr.
  - 2018-19: increased by 27.5% which is Rs.9429 Cr.
  - Now for 5 year: Rs. 50,000 Cr.
- The components of PMKSY scheme:
  - AIBP: Accelerated Irrigation Benefit Programme
  - PMKSY: Hark khet ko pani
  - PMKSY: Per drop more crop
  - PMKSY: Watershed development

OPERATION GREEN TOP TO TOTAL

- The scheme approved on 10th June, 2020
- Scheme guideline notified on 11th June, 2020
- Ministry of Food Processing Industries (MoFPI) has recently extended the Operation Green Scheme from Tomato, Onion and Potato (TOP) to all fruits and vegetables (TOTAL) for a period of six months for piolet basis as part of Aatmanirbhar Bharat Abhiyan

- Objective:

    - To protect the growers of fruits and vegetables from making distress sale due to lockdown and reduce the post-harvest losses

- Eligible crops:

    - Fruits- Mango, Banana, Guava, Kiwi, Litchi, Papaya, Citrus, Pineapple, Pomegranate, Jackfruit
    - Vegetables: French beans, Bitter gourd, Brinjal, Capsicum, Carrot, Cauliflower, Chilies (Green), Okra, Onion, Potato and Tomato
    - Any other fruits/vegetables can be added in future based on recommendation by Ministry of Agriculture or State Government

- Duration of Scheme: for the period of six months from the date of notification
- Eligible Entities: Food Processors, FPO/FPC, Co-operative Societies, Individual farmers, Licensed Commission Agent, Exporters, State processing/marketing of fruits and vegetables

- Pattern of Assistance: Ministry will provide subsidy @50% of the cost of following two components, subject to the cost norms:

    - Transportation of eligible crops from surplus production cluster to consumption center
    - Hiring of appropriate storage facilities for eligible crops

- Minimum quantity of crop to be produced and transported/ stored

    - 50 MT for individual farmers
    - 100 MT for FPO/FPC, cooperatives, Group of farmers
    - 500 MT for Food Processor, Exporter, Licensed Commission Agent
    - 1000 MT for Retailers, State Marketing/Cooperative federation

- Maximum admissible subsidy amount per applicant will be Rs. 1 Cr. During the entire period of 6 months.

FPO: Farmers Producer Organization

- FPO: Farmers Producer Organization
- Entity formed by primary producers
- FPO is combination of Cooperative (No profit and no loss) and Private company (more efficiency and profitability)
- FPO registered under companies Act Section 9(A)

- Signification:

    - Enhance income
    - Sharing of profit among members
    - Professionally managed
    - Best prices
    - Value addition

- In the year of 2018-19 Govt. gave two announcements to promote FPO:
- 5-year tax holiday
- Small credit guaranty set up
- In the year of 2010 there were 200 No of FPO and in the year of 2019 it was 4000.

- Concerns:

    - Finance: Due to lack of assets institution credit not given by bank
    - Initially facing operational challenges to regulate market
    - Lack of legal recognition

ATMA: Agriculture Technology Management Agency

- Agriculture Technology Management Agency
- ATMA is district level registered society which works to develop all the district level Agriculture stakeholder agency
- Launched during 2005-06

- At present, the scheme is under implementation in 684 districts in 28 States and 3 UTs in the country
- The scheme is supported by central government, The funding pattern is 90% by the central government and 10% by state government. The 10% state's share shall consist of cash contribution of the state, beneficiary contribution or the contribution of other non-government organization

- Objectives:

    - New initiatives reach to farmers
    - To distribute decision power to different district level
    - To increase farmers' involvement
    - To centralize government, semi-government and private institute that related to Agriculture development

- How to joint ATMA project:
- Interested 15 or more than 15 farmers can jointly register their group with specific name
- Group Fee: Rs. 10 (10*15)
- Registration Fee: Rs. 250

࿇

MSP: Minimum Support Price

- MSP is Minimum Support Price
- MSP is the rate at which the government buys grains from farmers
- MSP is fixed on the recommendation of the Commission for Agriculture Costs and Price (CACP) and last decision taken by Cabinet Committee on Economic Affair (CACP)
- 23 commodity covered in MSP: 14 kharif, 6 rabi, 3 other
- 7 cereals: Paddy, Wheat, Maize, Bajara, Jowar, Ragi, Barley
- 5 pulses: Red gram, Pigeon peas, Black gram, Green gram, Masur
- 7 oilseeds: Mustard, Groundnut, Soybean, Sunflower, Sesame, Safflower, Niger seed
- 4 commercial crops: Cotton, Sugarcane, Copra, raw jute

- High level committee on restructure of Food Corporation of India (FCI) headed by Shanta kumar, submitted report in Jan, 2015 that only 6% farmers get benefit of MSP
- The committee in turn based its analysis on the National Sample Survey Offices'(NSSO)
- Shanta kumar panel consider only paddy and wheat fo procurement by FCI

- Other organization for MSP collection:
- NAFED: for Chana, Tur, Moong, Groundnut, Mustard
- Cotton Corporation if India for Cotton
- Dairy co-operatives for Milk

- Sugarcane: It's pricing is governed by the sugarcane control order 1966 issued under the essential commodities Act. Which provides for the fixation of a Fair and Remunerative Price(FRP) for cane during every sugar year (Oct.- Sept.)
- The budget for 2018-19 announced the MSP would be fixed at 1.5 times of production costs for crops by Mr. Arun Jetli
- The CACP does not do any field survey itself. It makes projects using state wise, crop specific production cost estimated by Directorate of Economics and Statistics in the Agriculture Mnistry which generally available with three-year lag

- CACP decide three kinds of production cost for every crops:
- A2: Crop production cost
- A2 + FL: A2 + Family labor cost
- C2: A2 + FL + Land and fixed cost

- 2018-19 Arun Jetli promised 1.5 times of cost of production which is A2 + FL cost but M.S. Swaminathan committee and BJP government at the time of eliction promised to give C2 cost of production and 1.5 times of C2 cost

MIS: Market Intervention Scheme

- MIS is Market Intervention Scheme
- Similar to MSP, there is a MIS which is implemented on the request of state government for production of perishable and horticulture commodities in the event of fall in market prices
- MIS implemented in case of Apple, Garlic, Oranges, Grapes, Mushroom, Clove, Black peeper, Pineapple, Red chili, Coriander seed, Chicory, Onion, Potato, Cabbage, Mustard seed, Castor seed, Copra, Palm oil etc.
- Department of Agriculture and cooperation is implementing this scheme

e-NAM PORTAL

- National Agriculture Market
- Launched on 14th April 2016
- Small Farmers Agribusiness Consortium (SFAC) is the lead agency for implementing e-NAM under the aegis of Ministry of Agriculture and Farmers' Welfare, Government of India

- Objective:
- To provide competitive and remunerative price to farmers
- To integrating the existing mandis to "One Nation One Market" for Agricultural commodities in India

- The portal is available in English, Hindi, Gujarati, Marathi, Telugu, Bengali, Tamil, Odiya and Panjabi
- Mobile app also available
- Call center number for beneficiaries is 1800-270-0224
- The pan Indian electronic agri-produce trading portal reaches milestone of 1000 mandis across 18 States & 3 UTs
- With the overall success of 585 mandis in Phase 1 and future expanding its wings to integrate 415 new mandis in Phase 2, the e-NAM platform now has a total number of 1000 mandis across 18 states & 3 UTs
- More than 1005 FPOs have been registered on eNAM plateform and have traded 2900 MT of agri-produce worth Rs. 7.92 Cr

CHAMAN

- Co-ordinated Program on Horticulture Assessment and Management using Geo-Information
- Launched in the year of 2014
- Implemented by Delhi based Mahalanobis National crop forecast center

- Features:
- Output of 7 horticulture crops in 12 states
- Geo spatial studies conducted to boost horticulture
- Help horticulture sector to provide Nutrient rich crops
- Digital inventory of all horticulture zones
- Identify areas of high PH losses reduced by cold storage
- Manage inflection by providing accurate data of food stocks
- Aims to make use of Geo-informatics to help farmers and policy makers in government
- Remote sensing technique use
- Aqua horticulture
- Use of GIS and GPS in different schemes like PMFBY, PMKSY, Soil health card, RKVY

SOIL HEALTH CARD

- Theme: "Swasth Dharaa Khet Hara" – Healthy Earth, Green Farm
- Launched: 19 feb, 2015 at Suratharh, Rajasthan
- Soil health card is prepared in 14 local languages
- SHC mobile app also launched on World Soil Day
- It will contain the status of his soil with respect to 12 parameters, namely N, P, K (Macro-nutrient); S (Secondary-nutrient); Zn, Fe, Cu, Mn, Bo (Micro-nutrient) and pH, EC, OC (Physical Parameter)
- Soil samples will be drawn in a grid of 2.5 ha in irrigated area and 10 ha in rain-fed area with the help of GPS tools and revenue map
- Soil samples are taken two times in a year, after harvesting of Rabi and Kharif Crops respectively or when there is no standing crop in the field

KISAN CREDIT CARD

- The Kisan Credit Card (KCC) scheme was initiated in August 1998
- Eligibility: Minimum age: 18 years, Maximum age: 75 years
- Card valid for 3-5 years subject to annual review. As incentive for good performance, credit limits could be enhanced to take care of increase in costs, change in cropping pattern, etc
- Security, margin, rate of interest, etc. as per RBI norms. RBI has decided to raise the limit for collateral-free agriculture loans from Rs.1 lakh to Rs.1.6 lakh
- Crop loans disbursed under KCC scheme for notified crops are covered under Crop Insurance Scheme, to protected the interest of the farmer against loss of crop yield caused by natural calamities, pest attacks etc.
- The Kisan Credit Card also provides personal accident insurance that farmers can opt for under the insurance, they will get coverage of up to Rs.50,000 in the event of death while Rs.25,000 in the event of an accident resulting in disability
- The farmers get the short term loans up to Rs.3 lakh at reduced rate of interest at 7%. If the farmers deposit the loan amount on the due date, they get another 3% rebate in the interest rate. So the effective rate of interest would be only 4%
- The facility of Kisan Credit Card has been extended to fisheries and animal husbandry farmers to help them meet their working capital needs
- According to an announcement made on 26 August 2019, the RBI will be providing a 2% subsidy on the rate of farmers who are engaged in animal husbandry and fisheries via the KCC
- Farmers will be able to avail loans of up Rs.2 lakh with a concession interest rate of 7%
- An extra 3% discount on the interest rate will be provided to farmers who have been promptly paying their loans

PM-KISAN

- PM-Kisan Samman Nidhi Yojna (PM-KISAN) –provide direct income support to the farmers

- Launched date: 24th Feb, 2019
- Came in effect from 1st December, 2018
- Objective: To augment the income of farmers
- Not covered: Landless labor
- PM Kisan is a central sector scheme with 100% funding from GOI
- Under the PM-KISAN scheme, all landholding farmers' families shall provide the financial benefit of Rs.6000 per annum per family payable three equal installments of Rs.2000 each, every four months
- State Government and UT administration will identify the farmer family which are eligible for support as per scheme guidelines
- The fund will be directly transferred to the bank accounts of the beneficiaries
- The first instalment for the period 1st December, 2018 to 31st March, 2019 is provided financial year itself
- Total beneficiaries till now 11.5 Cr.
- The complete expenditure of Rs.75000 Cr. for the scheme will borne by the Union Government in 2019-20
- The scheme is extended to all farmers families irrespective of the size of their landholdings

- Eligibility:
- All landholding farmers' families, which have cultivable landholding in their names are eligible to get benefit under this scheme

- Exclusion:
- All institutional landholders
- Farmer families in which one or more of its members belong former and present holders of constitutional posts
- All serving or retired officers and employee of Central/State Government Ministers
- All persons who paid income Tax in last assessment year
- Tenant farmer or landless labors are not eligible
- Micro land holdings, which are not cultivable, are excluded from the benefit under the scheme
- Agriculture land being used for non-agricultural purpose will not be covered for benefit under the scheme

PM-KISAN MAANDHAN YOJANA

- PM Kisan Maandhan Yojna for old age farmers under which a farmer will get Rs.3000 per month when he/she attains the age of 60 years.
- The GOI has introduced an old age pension scheme for all lead holding Small and Marginal Farmers (SMFs), namely the Pradhan Mantri Kisan Mann-Dhan Yojana (PM-KMY)
- It is a voluntary and contributory pension scheme for the entry age group of 18 to 40 years.
- The scheme is effective from the 9th August, 2019.
- PM_KMY provides for as assured monthly pension of Rs.3000/- to all land holding small and marginal farmers (SMFs), whether male or female, on their attending the age of 60 years.
- The amount of the monthly contribution shall range between Rs.55 to 200 per month depending upon the age of entry of the farmers into the Scheme.
- Life Insurance Corporation of India (LIC) shall be the Pension Fund Manager and responsible for Pension Pay-out.

- Facilities:
- In case of death of subscriber before vesting date, the spouse of subscriber has an option of continuing the scheme by payment of remaining contribution under the scheme, provided she/he is not already an SMF beneficiary of the Scheme.
- In case of death of subscriber before vesting date, if the spouse does not exercise option of continuing under the scheme, then subscribers' contributions along with fund 6 interest earned or saving Bank Interest whichever is higher would be payable to the spouse under the scheme.
- In case of death of subscriber before last date, if there is no spouse, then subscriber' contributions along with fund interest earned or Saving Bank Interest, whichever is higher, would be payable to the nominee/s under the scheme.

- Exclusions:
- SMFs covered under any other statuary social security schemes such as National Pension Scheme (NSP), employees' state Insurance Corporation scheme, Employee's' Fund Organization Scheme, etc.

- Farmers who have opted for Pradhan Mantri Sharm Yogi Maan Dhan Yojana (PMSYM) administered by the Ministry of labour & Employment.
- All institutional Land holders
- Former and present holder of constitutional posts
- All serving or retired offers and employees of central/ state government ministries
- All persons who paid income tax in last assessment year
- Any individual farmer owing more than 2 hectare of cultivable land will not be able to get benefit under the scheme.
- Tenant farmer or landless labour are not eligible.

KCC

- Kisan Call Center
- Launched on: 21st Jan, 2004
- Toll free number: 1800 180 1551
- Timing: 06.00 AM to 10.00 PM
- Operation: 3 levels
- Total KCC: 21
- Total languages in which KCC operates: 22.

www.ingramcontent.com/pod-product-compliance
Ingram Content Group UK Ltd.
Pitfield, Milton Keynes, MK11 3LW, UK
UKHW022019190726
13853UKWH00005B/2006